THE DANCE OF ISAIAH

Published by
KINGS OF LUIGHNE PUBLISHING
10803 Adare Drive Fairfax VA 22032

Hara, Edward 1949 -

The Dance of Isaiah /Edward Hara
ALL RIGHTS RESERVED

I0132565

Kings Of Luighne
Publishing

Virtute et claritate

O'Hara

ISBN-13: 9780615556642

ISBN-10: 0615556647

Cover Photo: Icon of the Wedding At Cana. Thanks to Christ the Savior Orthodox Church in Harrisburg PA for permission to use.

THE DANCE OF ISAIAH

CORRECTING THE CALVINIST & EVANGELICAL UNDERSTANDING OF THE BIBLICAL COVENANT

CONTENTS

Preface and Forward

Page 1	In the Beginning – God is Covenant
Page 15	Love Creates Life – The Father and the Son
Page 27	Adam's Dead Family
Page 36	The Faithful Son –The New Family
Page 51	Restoring Our Mother
Page 64	The Language of the Family Redemption
Page 84	The Covenant Family at Worship
Page 109	Signs of the Covenant Family
Page 125	Justification – Entering & Staying in the Family
Page 144	Five Principles of a Covenant Family
Page 173	The Family Continues Forever
Page 184	Resistence is Futile – I Join the Family
Page 195	Some Answers to Common Questions
Page 208	Matthew 16, the Keys, and the Church

FORWARD

In the pages which follow, I offer to Orthodox Christians material which I hope will be helpful in your evangelization effort if you should find yourself someday in conversation with person who holds deeply to Covenant Theology. Most likely, this will be a member of a conservative Presbyterian organization such as the PCA or OPC.

There are many as different methods of evangelization as there are people. What might well be used of the Holy Spirit to bring the Gospel home to the heart of one individual might well turn another one off. Indeed, conversion stories I have read are filled with different experiences of how people came to Christ in different manners, through different approaches, and using different means. I hope this book will provide for my Orthodox brothers and sisters another tool in their efforts to evangelize and share the fullness of the Christian faith, which is the Orthodox faith, the faith of the Early Church.

I have found that for most Christians, bringing the Covenant of God into a theological conversation results in raised eyebrows and a look of confusion. Only in the Presbyterian Church in America did I encounter people such as Scott Hahn, for whom the covenant and its principles eventually led to his conversion to the Roman Catholic faith. A few years later, my study of these principles, explained in Ray Sutton's book, THAT YOU MAY PROSPER - Dominion by Covenant, led me to enter the Byzantine Catholic Church in April of 2001.

Unfortunately, at that time misapplied one of the five working principles of a covenant relationship, one which Scott Hahn also missed. I think this came from my being familiar with the Western churches of Roman Catholicism and Protestantism and the manner in which they approach Christianity. Over the last several decades, a growing number of Evangelicals and Protestants have discovered the beauty and fullness of the ancient Orthodox faith.

In the Orthodox faith, a theologian is one who prays, and one who prays is a theologian. Theology is not approached in the same manner as it is in the West, as an exercise of mental acuity, clever dissertations on God, and intellectual exercises done in regard to Bible passages, often clouded by the prejudice and judgment of the one reading the text. It is instead, coming to know Christ/God through prayer, ascetic exercise, and the silence of the heart before God, or heyschasm. It is to *experience* God, not just to talk about the ideas your own mind or your own understanding of the Bible have formulated about Him.

I am newly chrismated into the Orthodox faith, and while Eastern Catholicism tries to be Orthodox, it is not at all the same. In entering the Church, I made up my mind to sit down, shut up, listen, and learn. As such, I shouldn't even be writing this book, but there is a problem I need to address. After my conversion from Protestantism, I wrote and published the initial draft of this book, with the goal of sharing with friends and others the covenant principles which had led me to enter into communion with the Roman Catholic Church through Eastern Catholicism. This book is available on the open market, therefore, it needs to be revised and republished in order correct the error I made in the discussing Sutton's second principle of covenant – hierarchy.

Hierarchy is the principle of covenant headship. As you will see discussed later on, Christ is the New Adam, who is the human covenant head over the Church – not the Patriarch of Rome.

PREFACE

My life has been a long, winding, and sometimes quite mysterious spiritual journey. I have belonged to a variety of Christian denominations as I continued to study the Bible and seek greater understanding.

On April 14th, 2001, I left Protestantism to join St. Ann Byzantine Catholic Church in Harrisburg PA. After two years of intensive study of what I as a Protestant formerly regarded as "papist heresy," I felt at that time that I had found the apostolic church of the early fathers of Christendom and that my objections to anything Catholic were not grounded in a good realization of Christian history. All the anti-catholic prejudices which I had been taught over a period of years were destroyed by coming into contact with Roman Catholic apologists who charitably but nonetheless showed me the errors in Protestant thinking.

As a Protestant, I thought I knew a great deal about Christianity. I found instead that my knowledge was nothing more than the most abbreviated possible history one could possess, consisting of a smattering of knowledge about St. Augustine and the Nicene Creed. Had you asked me about the seven ecumenical councils of the Church, about St. Polycarp, St. Ignatius, or St. Irenaeus, I would have given you a quizzical look. Sadly, much of the more anti-Catholic Protestantism such as I practiced is built on this kind of misinformation, not only of Church history, but of God's dealing with mankind through the eternal covenant. Bluntly put, the covenant of God is the most misunderstood of all of the themes in the Bible, if it is even acknowledged at all. Most Christians get wide-eyed when a serious discussion of God's covenant comes up in conversation. It is not on their radar.

When I was first challenged by the Roman Catholic apologists whom I had met online, I began to read the books they recommended to me. I did so thinking that surely I would find the errors in their thinking and rip them apart, triumphing over my opponents in our Internet debate. As I read, I took the distinct doctrines of the Catholic faith and carefully applied covenant principles to them. These were principles I had learned in my Presbyterian assembly, and especially from the writing of Bishop Ray Sutton. [1] To my surprise, and not a little bit to my horror, the teachings of the Roman Catholic Church all appeared to fit into a covenant paradigm, even the ones I was sure were the most egregiously wrong, such as the honor given to the Blessed Virgin Mary. The covenant, properly understood, makes every Orthodox doctrine, and much of Roman Catholicism, fit the scriptures.

Yet now, after twenty years in the Byzantine Catholic Church, I have been chrismated into the Orthodox Church in America. When I was being catechized into the Byzantine Catholic Church, I was told that I could be "Orthodox in Communion with Rome." At that time, having little knowledge of Christian history or theology, this seemed an acceptable solution to my desire to be Orthodox, for I had found great beauty in the Orthodox Vespers I infrequently attended, and also to be under the one I mistakenly thought is the covenant head of the Church, the Patriarch of Rome. After years of further study, I have come to realize that this is both problematic and an impossibility.

---

[1] **THAT YOU MAY PROSPER** I Institute for Christian Economics I June 1987

To be "in communion" indicates a complete unity of dogma and practice, something which does not exist at this time between Eastern Orthodoxy and Roman Catholicism. This lack of unity is why Protestants are not allowed to receive the Eucharist in Roman Catholic and Orthodox churches. They do not accept or believe in that which Catholics and Orthodox believe. There is no theological unity, therefore, for a Protestant to partake of the Eucharist, which is the symbol par excellence of unity, would be to symbolize a falsehood.

In the same manner, trying to be Orthodox brought me into conflict with a number of major dogmas of the Roman Catholic Church which I, as a Byzantine Catholic, was expected to accept. These dogmas have no basis in the covenant of God. They are additions to the faith once delivered to the saints.[2] Things such as Indulgences, the Immaculate Conception, and the addition of the Filioque Clause to the Creed were not known to the Early Church. I have read a number of Roman Catholic apologists who have attempted to show that such dogmas belonged to early Christianity. I find their attempts lacking in both honesty and historical relevance. If they had a case, there would have never been the schism of 1054 AD when Rome left the unity of the Church.

I believe the principles of covenant which I wrote about in the first edition of this book apply to Orthodoxy with one very major exception – who is the Covenant Head of the Church on earth. In my untrained mind as a convert I thought that since the Church on earth is, as national Israel was, a body of human beings under a covenant headship, I assumed that there must be a human being as covenant head over the Church. My error was in failing to see Christ is that human being, the Last Adam, perfect man, and thus the human head over the Church, although not bodily present. That He has left for a time does not in any way suggest that someone else, the pope of Rome, has taken His place. Orthodoxy accepts the primacy of the Roman Patriarch. We do not accept him as head over the Church. There is a difference.

I initially wrote this book as an explanation I could give to Protestant

---

[2] Jude 1:3

friends why I left for Rome, and in particular to use the covenant of God as the reason. Now I am revising it to fit the covenant of God into the context of Orthodox theology. Perhaps it will help some Evangelical or Protestant seeker to understand why we do what we do in Orthodoxy. It also may show some true seeker in the Roman Catholic Church why they can come to Orthodoxy and be true to the teachings of the Early Church. There has been a steady stream of people leaving Roman Catholicism. I desire they find the fullness of the faith.

The catholic faith was defined by St. Vincent of Lerins as *"that which has been believed at all times, in all places, and by all people."* Thus, the faith of the united Eastern Western churches of the first eight hundred years of Christianity met that requirement. This united Church was catholic. It was one faith, dogmatically outlined by the Symbol of Faith – the Nicene Creed and the seven ecumenical councils. To this day, there is a similarity between East and West which is so close that Protestant outsiders consider us to be the same, not understanding the subtle differences in dogmatic approach. The Orthodox Church, under the definition of St. Vincent of Lerins, is Catholic. The church at Rome is not because she has added things that do not meet St. Vincent's requirements. Therefore, I am going to refer in this book to the church at Rome as the Roman Catholic Church and not just the Catholic Church to avoid confusion. Orthodoxy is the Church – one, holy, catholic, and apostolic. I do not apologize for saying this. [3]

While I have quotes from various sources in this book, one publication is referred to constantly. Ray Sutton's book, THAT YOU MAY PROSPER – Dominion by Covenant, is considered by many Reformed and Calvinist writers to be the best explanation of covenant principles contained within the Scriptures.

---

[3]

At the same time, let me say that I do not wish my Orthodoxy to be defined by being an anti-Roman Catholic bigot and hater. I have no doubt there are many in the Roman Catholic Church who love Jesus more and far better than I ever will. The errors of their church do not translate into me having the right to call them names or hate them. We have had far too much of that on both sides for the last two thousand years and it is a blot on the Christian faith. But at the same time, truth is important, and this book is, hopefully, an exposition of truth vs error.

Unfortunately, as you will see upon further reading, he has made a critical, but common, mistake in the Protestant view of the covenant of God. His principles are sound, but they are misapplied when thought to be legal rather than relational.

The publishing of doctrinal books by laymen is a perilous affair at best. Untrained in theology, it is all too easy in the zeal of the convert to step into areas in which we simply do not belong. It is my hope that what I have written here, and the changes made, will present the incredible beauty of the personal relationship which our covenant with Christ gives us through the universal, or catholic faith which Christ established to bless the world, and which the Orthodox Church has carefully maintained through the centuries.

Jer 31:13 Then shall the virgin rejoice in the dance, both young men and old together: for I will turn their mourning into joy, and will comfort them, and make them rejoice from their sorrow

IN THE BEGINNING – GOD IS COVENANT

Far too many people, especially in Western theology, interpret the Bible by proof-texting, which is the practice of using isolated quotations from a document to establish a proposition. When I was a Protestant, I followed right along with this established norm, quoting isolated and carefully chosen Bible verses as a solid defense of whatever belief system I was in at the time, all the while ignoring a deeper and more thorough study of the Bible as a whole. In short, I was an arrogant ignoramus who thought he knew everything about the Bible and the Christian faith. As I said earlier, what I knew about the Christian faith could have been put in a thimble and have had room for a Mack truck.

Proof-texting ignores the continuity of the Sacred Scriptures as a complete whole. In order to view the scriptures as a complete whole, it is necessary to be conversant with them from beginning to end, Genesis to Revelation. I believe that a lack of dealing with the Bible as a whole causes

Christians to fail to have a proper covenant framework. Yet the covenant of God is the overarching theme of the Bible and God's dealing with mankind. Rev. Ralph Smith states: *"The starting point for such an inquiry cannot be anything other than the biblical account of the creation, for the Bible itself emphasizes that how God created the world reveals what kind of God He is."* [4]

"The world of the Bible is a covenantal world. The doctrine of creation - fundamental to the Biblical doctrine of God no less than it is to the Biblical doctrines of revelation, history, man, sin, and salvation - introduces us to the covenantal theme from the very beginning of the Bible. Though the word "covenant" itself is not used in the creation narrative, covenantal ideas and vocabulary abound. Also, it is not, as is often mistakenly thought, that God created the raw stuff and then afterwards made a covenant. The point is rather that the act of creation itself was a covenantal act, bringing the world into existence as a covenantal world.

Thus, too, from the beginning God reveals Himself in the world and speaks to man as covenant Lord. It was not necessary for God to speak to Adam about making a covenant because the covenant relationship was already established by creation. God's words to Adam presupposed the covenant. And just as throughout the subsequent history of the world, God's relationship to man is always and only covenantal, God's word to man is always covenantal." [5]

It is important to know what is meant by Calvinists when they use the

---

[4]

Rev. Ralph Allen Smith I Eternal Covenant-How The Trinity Reshapes Covenant Theology, Page 14 I Canon Press I 2003

[5]

Covenant Worldview Institute, Trinity and Covenant, Rev. Ralph Allen Smith, http://www.berith.org/essays/tcv/tcv03.html

term "covenant" in relation to the Trinity. In Calvinist soteriology,[6] it is the understanding that the Father and the Son enter into an agreement for the salvation of a certain number of persons who are known as "the elect." Traditional Calvinist theology therefore is not speaking of the eternal covenant as the very state of being of the Trinity, a relationship of deep and complete union in love, but rather of a contract between the Father and the eternal Word. As I will mention further on, the wording of this agreement sounds like a contract instead of a relationship of love and unity.

I find another reason this is just weird to me. Agreements or contracts are entered into by two parties who don't trust each other fully. In a contract, both sides have their own self-interest first and foremost, and use the contract to be sure that they are not taken advantage of by the other party. How would the Father and Son need to enter into any sort of contract when there is not the slightest shade of variance between them in their love and unity? Father, Son, and Holy Spirit are one God, one mind, one unity and purpose.

Because we do not walk intimately with God as Adam did, to begin to have even a limited understanding of Him, we must use the analogies He has placed in scripture to convey truth about Himself, truth we would we would not be able to understand if we were able to see God in all His glory. God is unknowable in His fullness, not only here, but in eternity. Even the choicest of saints will never come to know the complete fullness of God. It is simply impossible for any creature to know essentially the One Who is. Therefore, in order to communicate some of His attributes to us, God uses analogies in the Sacred Scriptures.

Analogy:
a resemblance in some particulars between things otherwise unlike:

---

[6] **Soteriology is the study of salvation.**

similarity

b : comparison based on such resemblance [7]

Here is our first analogy from scripture regarding the covenant of God.

Ezek. 16: 8 Now when I passed by thee, and looked upon thee, behold, thy time was the time of love; and I spread my skirt over thee, and covered thy nakedness: yea, I sware unto thee, <u>and entered into a covenant with thee</u>, saith the Lord GOD, and thou becamest mine.

There are two primary analogies in scripture which help us understand God and our relationship to Him. One of them is the family. The other is that which is seen in Ezekial 16:8 – that of marriage. The same language "I spread my skirt over thee" is used in the story of Ruth and Boaz. This is the language of marriage – the beauty of two people *giving themselves completely and sacrificially to each other in love.* They make vows to one another and enter into a union of love. We seldom hear marriage described as "the covenant of marriage" anymore. But that is exactly what the deeply personal union of marriage is – a covenant. And family naturally derives from marriage.

A few months after I entered St. Ann's Byzantine Catholic Church I was invited to attend the marriage of two friends from my new parish. Since they were married in our Eastern Rite Catholic Church, this was an entirely new experience for me. I had never seen the beauty of the marital covenant expressed in such deeply symbolic acts. The entire experience was profoundly moving for me, but two events especially stood out for me in the way that they spoke to the

---

[7]

As we use the analogies of the Bible, it is important to remember that no analogy perfectly describes that which it is trying to represent. All analogies "limp," that is, they are imperfect in their effort to show us the fullness of the object they resemble.

covenant of God.

Jonathan and Mary [8] were brought to stand before the tetrapod [9] in front of the Iconostasis. [10] Upon their heads were placed crowns. Upon seeing this, the first thing which came to my mind was "King Adam and Queen Eve." As you read further in this book, you will come to understand the significance of what is being shown here. God is establishing a new covenant family right before our eyes. He is crowning a new covenant head over the family in King Jonathan and his helpmeet, [11] Queen Mary. But more than that, what I saw pictured was the first Garden marriage of Adam and Eve. Because of Christ's work upon the Cross, not only has the whole human race been returned to relationship with God through Christ, but every marriage is a symbol of that redemptive work being accomplished in the two who are being married. Jonathan and Mary will now go forth to accomplish in their little family the same thing which Adam and Eve were to accomplish – to bring forth sons and daughters of God who will be raised as covenant children for the kingdom. They, in turn, are a picture of the greater and larger family of God, the Church, established by King Jesus, Who is the Last Adam, and Queen Mary, who is the New Eve. With the crowns held in place, Father Mike led them around the tetrapod where the Holy Bible and symbols of marriage lay. Three times around this table he led them in the Dance of Isaiah. I could imagine myself suddenly back in Israel, seeing the couple dancing, perhaps a little more fervently than the crowns they

---

[8] Names changed to protect privacy.

[9] A small table in front of the altar on which are placed icons.

[10] The Iconostasis is a screen which separates the altar from the sanctuary where the faithful stand. It is decorated with icons of Christ, the Virgin Mary, and the saints

[11] The word "helpmeet" is of Old English derivation, meaning "a suitable helper."

were wearing would allow, round and round in joyous circles.

Later, I asked our parish cantor for a description of the Dance of Isaiah. This is what he wrote to me:

"In the Byzantine wedding service, after placing crowns on the heads of the bride and groom to seal their union with the gift of the Holy Spirit, the priest offers them a cup of wine to drink - a symbol of the one life they will now share. Then, the priest leads the couple three times around a table in the center of the church while special hymns are chanted - the same hymns that are sung at the ordination of a priest. This ritual dance is an icon of Christian marriage: led by Christ (represented by the priest), the couple enters ever deeper into the life of the Holy Trinity (signified by the triple procession), dancing with the Lord for all eternity (signified by the circle). The table around which they dance represents the table of their home – the symbolic altar of their shared daily life. The last hymn during this dance celebrates the fulfillment of Isaiah's prophesy: "Behold, a virgin is with child and shall bear a son, and shall call his name Emmanuel," a name that means "God is with us" (Isaiah 7:14). It is this Emmanuel, the Lord in our midst, who makes marriage become a sharing in the kingdom - in God's own life."

When this ended, Father Michael pronounced blessings upon the couple. Over Jonathan he prayed the blessing of Abraham, Isaac, and Jacob. Over Mary he prayed the blessing of Sarah, Rebekah, and Rachael. As he did, it occurred to me that this was in entirely in keeping with the Jewish roots of Christianity.

The children of any marriage covenant are born into an existing covenant relationship called "family." Each family has its own set of standards which vary from family to family. These rules are set before the children for their profit, and that the family might enjoy the best of family unity in love. A wise child, blessed with good parents, does not rebel against the good expressed in these ethical norms, but rather submits to them to receive the blessings of obedience.

The covenant relationship produces life. Just as it is inevitable that the union of man and woman (think back before contraception made sterility in marriage seem normal) should produce life, so the covenant of love between the members of the Godhead had to produce life. Union produces life, and God, by the very nature of Who He is in covenant between the members of the Godhead, creates. By His very nature, the one God in Trinity creates life. Life is the result of covenant union. This is why Christians must be pro-life. We reflect the life giving nature of our Trinitarian God. For a Christian sanction death or sterility [12] would be spiritual harlotry of the worst sort. It would be a complete failure to represent God's character. It is the gods of paganism that bring forth death.

In the covenant of marriage the bride and groom, on the day of their union, make vows to each other with the understanding that there is a certain boundary, which if crossed, will break this covenant and render it null and void.

Christ spoke of this boundary:

Matthew 19:9 And I say unto you, Whosoever shall put away his wife, except it be for fornication, and shall marry another, committeth adultery: and whoso marrieth her which is put away doth commit adultery.

Why only for this sin did Christ say that the wife may be put away? Because in the marriage covenant, man and wife are first pronounced one flesh, then they actually become one flesh in the nuptial bed, which is the sealing of the covenant. The Bible teaches that we become one flesh in the sexual act, therefore, when one has intimacies with another in adultery, he has broken the physical bond of unity which makes the covenant relationship real. Being harsh and mean with one's mate does not do this. It may make a spouse miserable to live with, but it does not break that unity by establishing unity with another. It does not destroy the physical reality of marriage which is so distinctly shown in the sexual union. The sexual union is the apex of the marriage covenant: man and

---

[12] Such as in abortion, contraception, or homosexual unions.

woman completely given to each other, body, soul, and spirit. The outward joining shows the inner commitment. Thus, the joining to another outside the bonds of marriage shows the turning away from the one committed to in the covenant of marriage. It is the ultimate betrayal by giving one's complete self to another.

This union of self-giving between two which brings forth a third is a shadow and type of the state of being between the Father, the Son, and the Holy Spirit. They are One, yet Three in One. We are given the bond of marriage as a pattern of the heavenly union of the Blessed Trinity. If you understand the positive good of marriage with its blessings and love, you can then transfer, *in a very limited way*, the truths you find there to the relationship the Godhead enjoys. This is why God said that it was not good that man be alone. It is because Adam alone would be no pattern of the divine covenant relationship between the persons of the Trinity and the sharing of love between them.

If the analogies of scripture show us anything at all about God, it is that not only is He a covenant Being, but that all His relationships are covenant relationships, both within the members of the Trinity and with mankind. Our Lord used the analogies of marriage, and the family that results from marriage, to make reference to God, heaven, and His dealings with us as His people. It is from this foundation of marriage that I will be making my case for covenant. Not as a contract, as do Calvinist theologians, but as family.

The first family reference to God goes back to Genesis. It is found in Luke 3:38, where Adam is called "the son of God." As I see it, this is a critical point of divergence between the traditional Protestant Calvinist understanding of covenant and the Orthodox understanding. Calvinism describes God's covenant relationship with Adam and mankind not in terms of family and Father, but in terms of King, Master, and Lord, which, while certainly true, do not adequately describe the love relationship between God and we His Creation, as sons and daughters who are beloved.

"It is clear that man's position is one of representative authority (Gen 1:26), for which man would have to give account (Gen 2: 15-17). Man is over the world as God's vice-regent, but under God's command and responsible to Him." [13]

In the Westminster Confession of Faith, and the writings of Calvinist clerics such as Sibbes, Rutherford, and Owen, to name a few, we find the same idea of man as vassal vice-regent. In Calvinist theology, it is not family and fatherhood, it is not love and union, but slaves under law,[14] which they consider to be the foundation of the covenant. Not surprisingly, Reformed thought is a veritable hotbed for a system of scripture exegesis known as "theonomy" (Theos = God. Nomos = law). The writings of such men as Gentry, Bahnsen, Rushdooney, North, see our relationship to God only through the lens of the keeping of God's Law. I remember very little being said in Calvinism regarding God as Father and His love for all mankind. Indeed, being good Calvinists, they absolutely do **not** believe God loves all mankind, but only loves a nebulous number of people known as "the elect."

For Calvinists, the defining sign of one being a true believer is not love, but how well one adheres to the demands of the Law of God. Perfect obedience, marked especially by being in agreement with all the dogmatic teachings of Calvinism, is considered sure proof you are of the elect and assured a place in heaven. Such understanding brings us right back to covenant as contract, and as a contract it must be kept perfectly. In my experience, there is simply no place for a father's grace or familial love and relationship.

---

[13] **Rev. Ralph Allen Smith | Eternal Covenant-How The Trinity Reshapes Covenant Theology, Page 35 | Canon Press | 2003**

[14] **"Covenant means law, law means obedience, and disobedience means judgment." | THAT YOU MAY PROSPER | Ray Sutton | Institute for Christian Economics | June 1987 | Page 27.**

10

A biblical covenant is not a legal piece of paperwork by which one makes demand upon the other. It is the relationship of two people who have given themselves without reserve to each other in marriage. Let us look again at the definition of covenant in the scriptures:

Ezek. 16: 8 Now when I passed by thee, and looked upon thee, behold, thy time was the time of love; and I spread my skirt over thee, and covered thy nakedness: yea, I sware unto thee, <u>and entered into a covenant with thee</u>, saith the Lord GOD, and thou becamest mine.

Look at the verse from Ezekiel carefully. Is this the language of a contract? I am hard pressed to think so when I see in scripture further explanations of the personal feelings which God expresses towards Israel as His bride. I hope as you read them you will see and feel the desire, the longing, and the care for Israel, the family of God, which is present in each of these verses:

Isa 62:5 For as a young man marrieth a virgin, so shall thy sons marry thee: and as the bridegroom rejoiceth over the bride, so shall thy God rejoice over thee.

How lovely! God rejoicing over Israel as a bridegroom rejoicing over his bride. Where is the sense of contract here? Where is the sense of servitude and vassal slavery which Calvinists insist is the rightful position of Adam and Eve as first created of humanity? I do not see it at all.

Isa 43:4 Since thou wast precious in my sight, thou hast been honourable, and I have loved thee: therefore will I give men for thee, and people for thy life.

This verse speaks of the love and desire of God for His Bride, which is His people, Israel. And when His people turn from Him, He uses the language of marital intimacy perverted to express that betrayal – whoredom. Spiritual infidelity is analogized as an act of sexual betrayal – the most intimate act which exists between a husband and wife being instead given to another who does not deserve it.

The Calvinist definition in the Westminster Shorter Catechism is totally devoid of relational intimacy. Listen to its language:

Q: WHAT IS A COVENANT?

A: AN AGREEMENT BETWEEN TWO OR MORE PERSONS.

That's it. Barren. There is nothing said about love between two persons. There is nothing which indicates the action of one giving one's self totally to the other. It is a legal contract and nothing more. As such, that definition is not a biblical covenant. In this Calvinist understanding, I find it hard to see God as either a father or a spouse. To actively damn some (reprobation) rather than to seek by all means to save them and bring them home does not strike me as the actions of the One who is called our Father. Everything in Reformed thought regarding mankind presents the relationship as that of a lawbreaker standing before a judge, a vassal before the king he has offended, a slave waiting for the punishment he richly deserves for running from the household. One is either 100% innocent or 100% guilty. It is black and white with no room for grace whatsoever. Everything about the Calvinist idea of God breaks the analogy we see in a good earthly father. Genesis introduces us to the story of a family – the family which is God. The story has no beginning because the story, if I can use that term, is the story of the eternal covenant family of Father, Son, and Holy Spirit, who create mankind in their likeness and image. This is language alien to Calvinist thought, yet it is the language to which the analogy of marriage points.

There is no greater fullness of self-giving love than takes place in the bridal chamber. What has been only a shared desire for full union now becomes that fully involved union of the whole person from both husband and wife. And from their union springs forth new life. God said of Adam "It is not good that he be alone." Why? Because God is not a monad. God exists in a life-giving, Trinitarian union, therefore, to be an icon of the Living God, it was necessary mankind be created in a similar fashion.

"If however, someone insists on denying that notions of a covenantal relationship among the persons of the Trinity, he will have to explain why it is that throughout all of history, pre-and post-fall, that there is no other means of interpersonal relationship between God and man except through a covenant. Where did this covenant idea come from and why does it dominate history so utterly? Unless the opponents of a Trinitarian covenant can offer reasonable answers to these questions, the weight of presumption falls on the side of those who see God's covenantal work in history as an expression of the fact that He is a covenantal God in eternity, that covenant in history manifests the covenantal nature of the triune God Himself." [15]

In the beginning, God. One God in three divine Persons, an eternal covenant of love, a union of complete self-emptying giving which is analogized in scripture for us as marriage and the union which comes with marriage, a complete and total union of two which produces life. How did the Reformers miss this?

To understand God as Father and mankind as His children, sets a proper foundation for our understanding of mankind in the Creation, in history, and

---

[15] **Rev. Ralph Allen Smith | Eternal Covenant-How The Trinity Reshapes Covenant Reshapes Covenant Theology, Page 35 | Canon Press | 2003**

especially as it relates to salvation. [16]

From understanding God as Father, we can then ask this question: what did God, as the Being of Trinitarian covenant love between three divine Persons, do in the Garden of Eden? What was His ultimate plan? Surely the Lord, who created this massive universe upon solid and discoverable laws and principles, did not place Adam and Eve in the Garden without having an ultimate purpose for their lives. To know this plan and the goal for them is to also know what God had planned for the entire human race.

This is where the Calvinist understanding of God's covenant once again falls flat on its face. Traditional Reformed Covenant theology sees the ultimate goal of history as being the glory of God through redemption of elect sinners who only deserve hell. [17] I am in agreement with those who say this is far too truncated an ideal of history's goal. The goal of history was the redemption of all that was lost in the Garden of Eden through the coming of the promised Redeemer. That magnificent goal, while indeed giving glory to God, is not limited to a small class of people known as "the elect" but rather to all mankind. A true father does not save a limited number of his children when he has the desire and ability to save them all, and has expressed the desire to do so. When I was a Calvinist, I used to puzzle over the verses in the Bible which state God's desire to save all mankind. That was at odds with the Calvinist paradigm and I couldn't reconcile the two. That was not my fault. It was the error of Calvinism which created the struggle in my heart regarding God's salvific intent for

---

[16] Calvinist anthropology describes a portion of mankind as "sons of the devil" as if created that way. This is entirely false, a complete covenantal misunderstanding of Christ's words in John 8.

[17] Renald E. Showers | There Really is a Difference - A Comparison of Covenant and Dispensational Theology | The Friends of Israel Gospel Ministry | 1990 | Page 20

mankind. God has saved all mankind, every one who has ever lived, [18] but whether that salvation will result in a state of bliss or chastising torment is determined by what we do with His offer of salvation while we are in our journey on earth.

SUMMARY

There is only one covenant, the eternal relationship of the members of the Blessed Trinity. That covenant brought forth life in a son who was placed in a Garden of Paradise. Because he was a son, there was no contractual relationship between Adam and God, but a filial relationship. Any attempt to define the covenant of God in terms of a contract or treaty lays a false foundation for understanding what the eternal covenant is and how it works. Children are never treated like slaves, even when they are disobedient and fail.[19]

From this initial failure to properly understand the covenant of God, we will see in the coming chapters that it must lead to the development of a faulty theology and a faulty soteriology. When one starts with a bad foundation, no matter how skilled the artisan, the outcome is not going to be right.

---

[18]

> Rom 5:18 Therefore as by the offence of one judgment came upon all men to condemnation; even so by the righteousness of one the free gift came upon all men unto justification of life.

[19]

> I believe the best example of this is the parable of the Prodigal Son. He was willing to become a slave after treating his father in a heinous manner, yet his father would have none of it, treating him as son by restoring him to full sonship.

LOVE CREATES LIFE –
THE FATHER AND THE SON

They are called Adam and Eve. Adam, meaning *"mankind."* Eve, meaning *"mother of all living."* They are the first parents of the human race. This first family is an icon of the heavenly family which is the Father, Son, and Holy Spirit. To properly understand what constitutes the Church and how God's salvation plan works, we need to begin here.

Lu 3:38 Which was the son of Enos, which was the son of Seth, which was the son of Adam, which was the *son of God.*

When I first really "saw" this verse, it stunned me. When we hear the term *"the* son of God" our immediate thought is of our Lord Jesus Christ. Yet here is the first man God created being called God's son! I believe this has tremendous ramifications for our entire understanding of God and how He deals with mankind. Of no other sentient creature is it said they are called "the son of God" as Adam was. True, angels are referred to as "the sons of God," [20] but Adam is set apart from them by one very specific difference. He is created not of pure spirit, as the angels are, but from the elements of the Creation, in the flesh of man, he is created. He is created for a distinctly different purpose in which the angels can never share. He is made in the image of God within the physical creation and to be a priest/king before Him.

Ge 1:26 And God said, Let us make man in our image, after our likeness: *and let them have dominion* **over the fish of the sea, and over the fowl of the air, and over the cattle, and over all the earth, and over every creeping thing that creepeth upon the earth. 27 So God created man in his own image, in the image of God created he him; male and female created he them.**

It is not said anywhere in Sacred Scripture that the angels in heaven enjoy such a privileged status. Nowhere is it said they shall be priests and kings unto God, nowhere is it said they will bear dominion over the creation and all in it. Adam is given a unique and wonderful gift. He bears the image of God and in doing so, bears the very authority of God over the creation.

This is the first place we need to work with the familial analogy which has been given to us. In the Bible, Adam is identified as son. As son, Adam is the son/prince of God, who is the great King. Adam's destiny is to be king over Creation and bear the crown rights as king. This is what the sons of kings do. They mature and become kings themselves. This was the glorious destiny Adam

---

[20] **Job 38: 7**

could have had. We understand this by taking human kingship and applying it to the Psalms which describes God as King.

In creation, God placed His son on earth as head of the family, with the command to "be fruitful and multiply." From Adam, God intended a family of priest/kings to rule over the creation and share in the great love of the Godhead – Father, Son, and Holy Spirit. Adam had before him the possibility of immortality as an inheritance. Before him lay the opportunity to share in the divine nature as a created being. As St. Athanasius said *"God became man that man might become god."* [21] Note that man does not become God with a capital "G." We *never* shall share in the essence of God. He Who said of Himself "I am that I am" shall always be transcendent to His creation. Yet at the same time, He gives to his new son and bride the promise of sharing in His divine nature.

It is here in the Garden where the Calvinist understanding of covenant begins to tilt off center. Calvinists are fond of speaking of a strange idea called "The Covenant of Works."

The idea of God entering into a covenant of works with Adam would be correct *if* Adam were nothing more than a vassal slave, a thing or object, who having personhood, was entrusted with vice-regency and given certain duties, with the promise of reward for obedience and punishment for disobedience. Vassal slaves do not have relationship to or intimacy with those who are their overlords. But Adam is far more than a vassal slave. He is a _son_. He is, in fact and according to Luke 3: 38, the son of God. Fathers do not make covenants with their children. The children are born into the pre-existing covenant of the husband and wife who have brought them into the world through their covenant of love. They become part of and share in the existing familial covenant of their parents.

---

[21] St. Athanasius, *De Incarnatione* or On the Incarnation 54:3, PG 25:192B;

I have six children. I have these children because my first wife [22] and I entered into a covenant relationship called marriage. When each of my children was born, in fact, whenever a child is born to any family anywhere, there was no need for a ceremony of covenant cutting to establish a relationship between the child and the mother and father. A child born into a family is automatically part of a familial relationship. It would be nonsense of a high degree to have a ceremony to have the child make covenant with his parents. The child bears the image of the father and mother and is intimately and essentially a part of them by the creative act of their love/union.

Following the family analogy seen in the Bible, Adam was created by the already existing covenant relationship which existed between the Persons of the Trinity. God is Father and He creates a son. That son is created into the already established relationship of the Blessed Trinity and in some way, was a partaker in the divine love. Adam did not share in the essence of the transcendent Godhead, nor would he ever attain such a reality of being, but just as we are called to share in the very nature of God, [23] Adam, by dint of being son of God, was able to have a deep and profound relationship of love with God such as children have with their parents. I do not think it a stretch to say that it was intended that this relationship grow and deepen over the eons of time, just as such relationship between earthly parents and children grows.

There are some more modern Reformed writers who are getting onboard with this understanding, such as Rev. Ralph Smith. Where the older Calvinists wrote more in line with a strictly barren and contractual understanding of the relationship between Adam and God, Smith says the following:

"Covenant expresses the goal of all creation because man, God's

---

[22] **Karen Lynn Musser. + 2006 Eternal Memory!**

[23] **2 Peter 1: 4**

representative and image, is destined to be <u>covenantally one with God</u>, sharing in the fellowship of love that is the life of the Trinity from all eternity." [24]

Smith's understanding is a refreshing change from the idea of traditional Calvinism in which no mention was ever made (at least, not that I heard when I was a Calvinist) of being one with God or sharing in the divine nature, which is love.

Here is a statement of the more traditional Calvinist description of the "Covenant of Works." See if you can spot one very telling little word in it which shows us the Calvinist understanding of Adam as merely vassal slave:

"The Covenant of Works, also known as the Edenic Covenant, is the covenant that God had with Adam in the Garden of Eden where Adam would maintain his position with God through his obedience to the command of God to multiply and fill the earth, subdue it, and also not eat from the Tree of the Knowledge of Good and Evil."

Do you see it? The word is "position," found on line three. Adam did not have a position. Slaves and serfs have positions. Bosses and owners give me my position in a corporate setting. Here is another quote from a Calvinist which shows this same idea:

"Some scholars see in the covenant of works a form of what is called a suzerain-vassal covenant. In these types of covenants, the suzerain (i.e., king or ruler) would offer the terms of the covenant to the vassal (i.e., the subject). The

---

24

Rev. Ralph Allen Smith | Eternal Covenant-How The Trinity Reshapes Covenant Theology, Page 59 | Canon Press | 2003. Notice that Smith, as close as he gets in his understanding, still fails to describe Adam as son of God and therefore draw the proper conclusion as to why mankind can enter into this covenant of love with the Trinity. Vassal slaves do not have such privilege.

suzerain would provide blessing and protection in return for the vassal's tribute. In the case of the covenant of works, God (the suzerain) promises eternal life and blessing to mankind (the vassal represented by Adam as the head of the human race), in return for man's obedience to the stipulations of the covenant (i.e., don't eat from the tree)." [25]

Adam was no vassal! The Bible describes Adam as the *son* of God! Do not forget that! Sonship and family relationship set the tone for everything which comes after the Garden of Eden!

" The rewards we will receive from God in heaven are also acts of grace. They are God's crowning of His own gracious gifts. Had Adam been obedient to God's covenant of works, he would only have achieved the merit that comes by virtue of fulfilling the covenant agreement with God. Because Adam fell into sin, God, in His mercy, added a new covenant of grace by which salvation became possible and actual." [26]

Calvinist writer R. C. Sproul also makes the traditional mistake of all Calvinist theologians in not seeing Adam as son. Therefore, he describes the reception of eternal life as a reward of merit rather than the inheritance that it is. Slaves are given rewards by their masters. Good and productive servants receive rewards for work well done. But sons receive inheritance by virtue of being family and remaining in a relationship of love and honor with the father. My children do not have to merit my love. They may lose certain blessings because of disobedience, but they never stop being my children nor do I stop loving them.

---

[25] **Excerpt from "GotQuestions.org"** | What is Covenant Theology? | S. Michael Houdmann

[26] **Excerpt from "Essential Truths of the Christian Faith"** | R.C. Sproul | Tyndale House Publishers, Inc. | February 1998

I have every right to use this familial image because the scriptures do when they describe Adam as the son of God.

Notice also how Sproul goes on to describe God as supposedly instituting another covenant, the Covenant of Grace. One error leads to another. There is no such thing as the Covenant of Grace. It is a fond Protestant invention not supported by scripture.

"Jesus is the first person to get into heaven by His good works. We also get into heaven by good works—the good works of Jesus. They become "our" good works when we receive Christ by faith. When we put our faith in Christ, God credits the good works of Christ to our account. The covenant of grace fulfills the covenant of works because God graciously applies the merit of Christ to our account. Thus by grace we meet the terms set forth in the covenant of works." [27]

As error leads to error, Sproul falls deeper into the pit he has dug for himself. No man can make covenant for another man. To say the merits of Christ are applied to our account is to deny we must personally enter into our own covenant relationship with God, coming out of service to sin and covenanting ourselves to Christ. All covenant principles apply in this, including and especially the taking of vows. Christ corporately re-establishes mankind's relationship with God in the New Covenant, and we, in turn, are invited to become part of this New Covenant by entering covenant with Christ through baptism. Christ is called our bridegroom and we are described as the bride of Christ. As we enter our covenant with Him, by virtue of union with Him, we become a family member in the covenant which He has with God on behalf of all mankind.

---

[27] **Ibid**

The bridegroom wording points to the fact that we do not make covenant with God, but rather with Christ. For mankind's salvation, no man can make covenant with God except Christ, and no one makes covenant with Christ for my salvation except me. We do not enter into Christ by faith alone (yet another false Protestant doctrine). We cut covenant with Christ as our divine bridegroom, which means that we perform a covenant cutting ritual, and we become His bride. The analogy of the marriage covenant comes into play here with the words "bride" and "bridegroom" used to describe our relationship to our Lord. Since He is in union with the Father, as long as we remain in covenant with Him, we remain in the Father's household and share in all the blessings of the covenant family which is the Trinity.

When the Bible speaks of covenant, it is speaking of one covenant. The one and only covenant is the eternal relationship of the Trinitarian Godhead. It is that covenant relationship, and the relationship of love/union, into which we are adopted as sons and daughters. There is the familial imagery again!

I have heard a well-known conservative radio talk show host for many years use the phrase "words mean things." How often are we guilty of not paying close attention to the words of the Bible and instead reading into a verse or section a meaning of our own choosing?

Gen. 6:18 But with thee will I establish my covenant; and thou shalt come into the ark, thou, and thy sons, and thy wife, and thy sons' wives with thee.

Notice what God says about the covenant relationship he is about to establish with Noah. It is not a new covenant. God does not say "I will establish *a* covenant with you," as if the Noahic covenant is something entirely new and different. He says to Noah, "I will establish *my* covenant with you." The language presupposes an already existing covenant which is called "my covenant." It is, in fact, the same covenant which existed when Adam was created. It is the relationship/union of the Trinity which was first extended to Adam and now is extended to one of Adam's sons. God now recognizes the family relationship He has with Noah and establishes Noah as covenant head to lead the earthly family after the deluge.

My oldest daughter has four children. Do they have to establish a relationship with me, or are they ever related to and in covenant with me through being children of my daughter? They are and always will be my grandchildren. In a family relationship there are privileges which do not belong to any other child on earth. And when they have children, if I should live that long, I will have a special relationship with those children. There is no generational separation. There would be no need for them to come to me and ask to establish a family relationship with me. They do not have to cut covenant to be part of my relationship to my daughter. If I could live for a thousand years, every generation of children from my daughter onward would have covenant relationship to me.

I remember when I was in Bob Jones Fundamentalism, I heard more than one Fundamentalist preacher state, "God has no grandchildren!" Oh, but I beg to differ. If Adam is the *son of God,* and we the human race are the children of Adam, then we are indeed all the grandchildren of God the Father. There is a real truth that all human beings are His children, and in a much deeper and more profound way than the generality of saying all belong to God because He created all. Created objects belong to their owner but are not beloved. God loves all because all are His sons and daughters, not vassal slaves.

The sons of Adam were also sons of God. They were also part of the earthly covenant family with God as Father, even though the disobedience of Adam had created a separation between God and His family, mankind. God is moving to Noah to head up His earthly family because Noah is also a son of God by being son of Adam. What then is God doing by saying He will establish His covenant with Noah, and by extension also with Moses, Abraham, David, and ultimately with Jesus? I believe a case can be made that in Noah, God was establishing another Adam, a covenant or federal head to lead the family of mankind. Here is the scripture that seems to point to this:

1Corinthians 15:45 And so it is written, The first man Adam was made a living soul; the last Adam was made a quickening spirit.

Jesus is the Last Adam. Note carefully again the use of the word "last" in this verse. Jesus is not called the Second Adam, but rather the Last Adam. I believe this points to the existence of other men who were representationally called Adam. Adam was the positional and representational head over creation. This is where I made my mistake in understanding the covenant headship over the Church. Adamic headship is clearly outlined in this verse, and it points to Christ, not the Patriarch of Rome! My mistake!

In the course of time, though, because of man's fallen nature, creation became so corrupt that the Lord repented of his creating man and He was grieved in His heart. God determined to destroy His creation, but Noah found grace in the eyes of the Lord. God is ever-faithful, and there was still one of the line of Adam who was faithful to Him; He would not destroy all of creation while there was still one with whom He was in covenant union.

Why is this? Because the covenant of God was not just with Adam as created son. It was with all creation, therefore, if there was but one man left who could be covenant representative between creation and God, God in love would seek to avoid completely destroying His creation.

God called Noah to build an ark to house a remnant of all flesh, to begin creation anew once He had executed judgment on all sin that had corrupted the earth. God provided Noah with instructions for the building of the ark, how the animals were to be included, and the food to sustain them all, and when the time came for Noah and his family, and all the animals that were called by God, to enter the ark, they did so, and He shut them in. That is covenantal faithfulness and trust. Months later, when the flood waters finally receded, and all the earth was cleansed of the wickedness which had prevailed upon it, the ark was opened and creation's remnant debarked.

Noah then built an altar and renewed God's covenant with the sacrifices he made on it. As a sign (token) of the renewal of His covenant with Noah, and his descendants, and with every living creature that came out of the ark, God enlarged the conditions of his covenant by His promise to never again destroy the earth through flood, and set His rainbow in the clouds as the visual, representative promise that He would never do so again.

The Flood is covenant judgment falling upon the wicked, covenant blessing coming upon faithful Noah, and the restoration of the covenant that already existed by the offering of a sacrifice to renew the covenant. There is nothing of a new and different covenant here, only cleansing and continuation of the one and only covenant. There is also a new promise added to the covenant – I will not destroy the world in this way again.

Who was the first Adam? As the first son of the family, he was covenant head over mankind, which also gave him authority over all Creation. I believe this is what God was doing with Noah. God's actions renew the covenant after the cleansing of the flood. They say to Noah, as the patriarchical head over those who remain of mankind, "You are the one now who is over all things. You are the covenant head." As the covenant head and visible representative of that authority, Noah offers sacrifice. Yet in Noah, as with all who came after him, God could not find a perfect man to be the head of a new covenant which would supercede the old in perfection. Noah would fail.

Who is Jesus the Christ as Adam? He is the perfect man who is covenant head over the redeemed human race and redeemed creation. I believe what God was doing with Moses, Abraham, and David, was to offer an opportunity to be that perfect man, keep His covenant without failure, and thus do what Christ

Jesus actually did accomplish, to restore permanent covenant headship over the redeemed human race. The covenant family would be restored as in the Garden of Eden, and man would be put back into the eternal destiny lost in Adam. It is a restoration of the covenant headship of a son, forfeited by Adam's disobedience. None of the others who came after Adam were able to do this until Christ Jesus came and as man perfectly obeyed His Father, even unto death itself. God establishes His covenant relationship with Noah – and Noah fails. God establishes His covenant relationship with many who come after Noah – and they all fail. Until Christ. He keeps the covenant perfectly, offers the perfect and eternal Sacrifice upon which the covenant relationship of God and mankind is renewed forever as the New Covenant.

It is one covenant, one family, one inheritance which is eternal life. The obedient son, Christ Jesus, has restored the covenant, redeemed mankind, and opened the gates of Paradise for all who choose to enter in by way of cutting covenant with Christ.

SUMMARY

Adam failed as God's son. Like the Prodigal Son of the NT, his actions broke the relationship he had with his Father. In some way mysterious to us, he brought upon himself and his progeny a change which made it impossible to be in the presence of his Father. But he did not stop being a son. The family of God continued on earth in a state of separation from the Father's house. The promise was given that one day there would be a Son who would restore all things by His covenant obedience.

ADAM'S DEAD FAMILY

It is with Genesis we see the first of the Calvinist errors regarding mankind. This first error is the "T" of the well-known Calvinist acronym TULIP – Total Depravity. In Calvinist anthropology, man is not merely damaged by the fall, he is totally and completely dead. Because he is dead, man cannot do good. Thus, because he is dead and therefore unresponsive to God, in Calvinism he is described as being totally depraved.

Calvinists will no doubt respond this is indeed what is meant by death; we lose our free will and no longer bear God's image in this way. They are fond of pointing to physical death in the earthly realm and transposing the image of earthly death onto man's spiritual relationship to God. In doing so, they insist that by following the type we have in physical death, all mankind has no spiritual will at all, no ability to do good in God's sight. As one rather well-known Dutch Calvinist was fond of saying on his radio program when he was alive, *"Man in*

28

his natural spiritual state is a stinking, rotting corpse. " [28] But there's only one problem – it doesn't fit the scriptural definition of death we have in Luke 15: 10-32. It is one of many fond inventions of Calvinism.

For a Biblical definition, let us look at verse 32:

Luke 15:32 It was meet that we should make merry, and be glad: for this thy brother was dead, and is alive again; and was lost, and is found.

Notice the Prodigal is described by his father as having been dead, even though all through this parable he was very much alive and breathing. Seeing God uses words carefully and for a purpose in scripture, should we not then exegete within the parameters which God gives us and not go beyond those boundaries? If dead in this parable does not mean insensate, a stinking, rotten corpse, then what other understanding could it have?

Genesis 2:17 But of the tree of the knowledge of good and evil, thou shalt not eat of it: for in the day that thou eatest thereof thou shalt surely die.

And what happened on the very same day?

Genesis 3:23 Therefore the LORD God sent him forth from the garden of Eden, to till the ground from whence he was taken.

Adam was ***separated*** from the presence of his Father in the very same way the Prodigal was separated from his father when he pursued sin. Death in the scriptures refers to separation – not cessation of being, nor of thought, reasoning, and use of the will.

---

[28] Harold Camping, whose fallibility as an interpreter of scripture is shown in his two utterly failed prophecies of Christ's return in 1994 and 2011.

The Garden of Eden was the presence of God to Adam and Eve. Outside of this Garden lay a wilderness of pain and sorrow – outside the presence of the living God. This is another example of life being the icon of heavenly truth, for outside of union with God there is no life. God is life. We see this in the description of final glory in the book of Revelation:

Revelation 22:14 Blessed are they that do his commandments, that they may have right to the tree of life, and may enter in through the gates into the city. 15 For <u>without</u> are dogs, and sorcerers, and whoremongers, and murderers and idolaters, and whosoever loveth and maketh a lie.

The tree of life is in the city where God is. Life is found only in the presence of God, and outside of his presence is no life. Separation from God is death. But is it not cessation of consciousness. Not according to Christian orthodoxy. A corpse has no consciousness and therefore no ability to exercise its will. To say man is a spiritual corpse is to say we have no ability to exercise our will. Yet not only does scripture state that the grace of God appears to all mankind, but all are called upon to make the choice for life instead of death.

To stay consistent with their interpretation of the word death, Calvinists should be annihilationists. They should believe that man has a complete cessation of consciousness and will remain so in eternity, similar to what the Jehovah Witnesses believe. I have never met one yet who thinks this way. For some reason, they are totally willing to imagine that a man, who they claim is spiritually dead and insensate and never brought to life by God in this life, instead of being totally annihilated by continuing in such a state of unconsciousness and inability, is suddenly brought to life at the Last Judgment in order to put to eternal death.

Do you see the strangeness of that position? They are willing to take the soul from a state of being spiritually insensate and insist it experiences the new birth after physical death, which then makes it not a recipient of grace, but an inheritor of hell. I find that odd.

I must insist on the Biblical definition of death, which is separation from the presence of God. Separation from the kingdom household in which life and joy and love live. That is truly death. That is what was suffered by Adam in the day in which he sinned and broke the family covenant. As a son, he was sent out from the palace of the Great King. In keeping with the familial analogy, I think of it as being allowed to remain on the grounds, but the banquet room was closed to him, the presence of the Father denied, and the joys of intimacy severed. In a sense, he was sent out to the slave quarters, for he, and his family, became slaves of sin. But not without a promise that someday, the Father would rectify this situation and redeem everything which had been lost.

Finally, why did Adam and Eve suffer this result from their sin? Was it because God couldn't forgive them? Knowing the mercy of God, we know there must be more than this.

It appears to me that it was because when Adam, who was ruler of the world as prince, obeyed the Evil One, he turned the authority and rulership of this world over to him. We see this from a passage in the New Testament:

John 12:31 Now is the judgment of this world: now shall the prince of this world be cast out.

Jesus calls the Evil One the prince of this world. Who was initially created as the prince of this world? As the son of the King, it was Adam. But the act of obedience which Adam gave to Satan in some way forfeited his authority to the evil one and caused Adam and Eve to be banished from the Garden, stripped of the rulership over Creation.

Now we begin to see glimmers of the plan of God which began in Genesis after the Fall. The whole salvific plan of God was to restore the original order of the human family, and the rulership of mankind over Creation. The picture of this is the Father grieving over His lost son, but at the same time, bringing forth a plan to one day restore Man, His son, to rulership and glory!

Is man totally depraved and totally unable to do any good thing at all? Scripture once again shows Calvinism to be wrong in this also, and it does not take long at all for this to come to the forefront of the scriptures:

Genesis 7:1 And the Lord said unto Noah, Come thou and all thy house into the ark; for thee have I seen righteous before me in this generation.

Is this somehow a mistake in the Bible? The Lord says He has seen Noah as a righteous man in this generation. How can that be when Calvinism teaches the only thing man can do is evil, and he is totally corrupt in all his deeds? [29]

Continued study of the Bible gives us many verses in the OT which describe certain men and women as righteous because of what they do. James clearly says by works a man is justified and not by faith alone [30] It seems Calvinists suffer from a kind of presuppositional blindness when they come to verses like these in the Bible. I know how that works. I am amazed at the verses I never saw when I was reading the Bible as a Calvinist.

But more than just the problematic anthropology created by this first of Calvin's five errors, the idea of total depravity creates a serious problem with the principles of covenant and covenant keeping. Scripture presents a covenant as an intimate union which is analogized by marriage:

Ezek. 16: 8 Now when I passed by thee, and looked upon thee, behold,

---

[29] "The will is so utterly vitiated and corrupted in every part as to produce nothing but evil" (Institutes, Bk. II, Chapter II, Para. 26).

[30] James 2:24 One of the more ignored and despised verses of scripture to those who hold to the idea that man cannot be righteous by what he does.

thy time was the time of love; and I spread my skirt over thee, and covered thy nakedness: yea, I sware unto thee, and entered into a covenant with thee, saith the Lord GOD, and thou becamest mine.

And thou becamest mine. When I read this, I can almost hear the joy of the bridegroom as he delights in the prize which is his beloved bride. Such a union comes about when both parties freely and of their own desire, enter into this most intimate of unions.

In his book, Bishop Ray Sutton gives five principles of a covenant. These are presented as principles of Suzerainty kingship treaty/covenants, however, I am going to attempt in this book to show them as having application to the true covenant between man and God, which is seen in the Bible as the marriage covenant. In order for there to be covenant, these principles must be present. Take any one of them out and you no longer have a covenant. Please look at and remember these principles. They will be the focus of our discussions.

Transcendence - The greater offers covenant to the lesser.

Hierarchy - Who is in charge here?

Ethics - What are the rules (law) of the covenant I am entering into?

Oaths & Sanctions - Solemn vows taken by both parties.

Succession - The covenant continues from generation to generation.

The Calvinist idea of man as dead and unable to respond at all to God because of the fall means that man for his part would not be able to make vows under principle four of covenant. Yet for there to be a marriage, both parties must choose each other in love, respond to each other in love, and vow fidelity to each other, based on the ethics they both agree to. How then can a corpse make vows? How does a corpse enter into a covenant relationship which depends upon the mutual decision of both parties to enter the union?

The Calvinist answer to this dilemma is two-fold: they insist God first gives the corpse life, then as a result, the now no longer dead soul responds in the only way it can respond, by entering into the covenant relationship, which is the fourth part of the TULIP equation, irresistible grace. They also state that in the covenant between the Father and Christ, Christ does all the work of covenant keeping for mankind, since mankind can do nothing but evil, even as believers. This work of covenant keeping is then imputed to us so that we are seen as covenant keepers, even though we are not and cannot be according to Calvinism.

Here's the problem. If it is irresistible grace, a call that can only have one response which is pre-programed to be yes, then it is not a decision made of free will. In turn, if not a decision of free will, then it cannot be anything analogous to marriage. To fit the marital paradigm, the soul must choose of its own volition, just as a woman responds of her own volition with either a yes or no to the offer of marriage from the man. And if it is a covenant, no other person can keep on my behalf the vows I make The Calvinist understanding of man's condition after the fall does not fit the requirements of a covenant relationship..

It is said that Luther's personal analogy of mankind was of being snow covered dung heaps. Dung heaps are far from anything which God could care for in an intimate and fatherly way. When God created mankind, He proclaimed man to be good, the same statement He had made with all else He had created. Mankind did not cease to be intrinsically good upon the sin of Adam. There is nothing in the Genesis account in which God declares of man what Luther declared of mankind – a worthless mass of dung. I challenge the Calvinists who hold to the notion of total depravity to show me any passage in Sacred Scripture which indicates mankind suddenly lost the image of God and ceased to be God's sons. And since you are sola scriptura as to God's truth and revelation to mankind, I want to see a very clear reference verse relating to the image of God in man being either taken away or lost by the Fall.

Save your time. It does not exist. In fact, it cannot be found except by the

34

most tortured of reasoning and twisting of scripture. Adam did not cease to be God's son. Therefore, neither did the entire human race contained within his loins yet unborn.

When the Fall took place, the nature of mankind became corrupted and turned to self-seeking rather than self-giving, which is the nature of God. This corruption of his very being is at the heart of why there could no longer be a covenant relationship between God and man. Mankind – male and female – now would only seek to take. Mankind could not share in the divine nature, which is of love and self-giving. It was not a legal violation but rather an ontological change by which man could no longer have a relationship with God. The natural condition of man was now in a state of antagonism to the presence of God and having a self-donative relationship with Him.

Because of this corruption of the person, mankind was banished from the Garden of Eden, the rightful home in which he should have enjoyed God's presence and unitive love. In the state he was in, he would have been unable to participate in a relationship of complete self-emptying and being filled by another. The merest glance at history shows us mankind consistently taking from others. Pagan civilizations, untouched by the Holy Spirit, are filed with stories of men taking violently from other men. If allowed to continue, by eating from the Tree of Life, this violent rejection of self-giving, divine love would have been the eternal state of man, something which could not have been present in the beauty of heaven's self-giving love.

So now we have a family separated. The son/prince of the Garden of Eden is driven from his father's household because in his sick state, with his nature diseased by sin, he cannot live in the same house with his Father. He is sent into a selfish wilderness of evil, sorrow, and pain, and like the Prodigal Son, leaves to wallow in a pig stye of immorality and filth. All his children, generation after generation, are born into a world in which there is a consequence of this broken covenant relationship. Unlike Catholicism, the Orthodox faith does not believe in Augustine's idea of Original Sin whereby all are born bearing the guilt of Adam. But all are born into the consequence of sin, which is death. And the state of death, separation from God, manifests itself in the corruption of our nature and the propensity to sin.

By the time our reading of the Bible comes to Genesis 6, so pervasive is the horror that sin has plunged the world into that God repents of creating mankind and sees the only solution is to purge the earth of the violence and sin by the Flood.

Yet a wonderful promise has been given earlier, a promise of a restoration of this family by the coming of one who will crush the serpent's head. My desire is to show you how that family has been restored through the One Who is the Last Adam and how He established a new family on earth – one, holy, catholic, and apostolic.

SUMMARY

The result of Adam's sin is a dead family. Not dead in the sense we understand an earthly corpse – insensate and unable to respond to stimuli – but rather separated from life. Separated from God, Who is life. The result of this Fall from filial relationship with God has the effect of distorting man's nature so that we can no longer be in unity with our Father. We are sick and cannot cure ourselves. In addition, it appears from scripture that in some way, the evil one has usurped Adam's place, being called "the prince of this world." All of this must be redeemed and set aright.

THE FAITHFUL SON –
THE NEW FAMILY

Going back to Genesis, we see one of the things which appeared to be in the plan of God was His desire to have a family of flesh and blood on earth. It was to be a representative family in which Adam represented God to Creation and Creation to God. This family began with His son, Adam, and the son's wife, Eve. The children who would have come from this union would in turn have also been born princes and princesses.

God placed His newly created son in the Garden. He brought unto Adam a helpmeet by which Adam, in loving covenant union with his spouse, would pattern his heavenly Father by bringing forth life through their union. Adam was to be a priest/king in the Garden, acting as an intermediary between God and the Creation He had made. That is what a priest does. That was Adam's destiny, and much more. The covenant Adam was created into was simple. He was given positive direction, [31] which was to bear his Father/King's authority over all the earth, and a negative to obey.[32] Both of these commands were there to establish his relationship with God as an obedient son. They were not laws. Relationships do not work by the use of laws and legal framework. They were the desires of the Father by which Adam could express his love for his Father through obedience.

A glorious future awaited Adam. He was a prince, the son of the great King of the universe, and one day could rule as king himself. But in what may seem to be a paradox, in order to achieve this end, it appears to me it was necessary Adam be tested.

It is an interesting thing to think about, and more than one Christian over the centuries has pondered over the question: *"If God is all powerful, why did He allow the devil into the Garden to tempt Adam and Eve so they might fall?"* I think I may have an answer to this. It is my opinion – and only an opinion, please – that it was for the purpose of them growing in righteousness.

The new prince and princess of Creation were not created righteous. They were created innocent. Free of guilt and stain, they needed to grow, like all newborns, in that very quality which makes us bear the image of God, self-giving, self-sacrificial love. Without this growth, they would have remained mere spiritual babies. Such was never God's plan. To make full grown, mature sons and daughters out of us, God does with us the same thing that He did with Adam and Eve, He permits us to be tested. The result of our testing is either sin (disbelief, lack of faith) or righteousness (faithful trusting), depending upon our response to the trials which come into our lives.

---

[31] Genesis 1: 28 Be fruitful, and multiply, and replenish the earth, and subdue it: and have dominion over the fish of the sea, and over the fowl of the air, and over every living thing that moveth upon the earth.

[32] Geneis 3: 3 But of the tree of the knowledge of good and evil, thou shalt not eat of it.

38

Ro 4:13 For the promise, that he should be the heir of the world, was not to Abraham, or to his seed, through the law, but through *the righteousness of faith.*

Faith is righteousness.[33] Only through the exercise of faith do we grow in righteousness. Every exercise of faith is an exercise in growing in righteousness. The deeper the testing, the more we grow in righteousness, providing we pass the test by acting in faith in God despite our circumstances.

Imagine a scenario of Genesis 3 different than what took place. I think the following could have happened. Rather than submitting to the evil one, Adam resists the devil. Some theologians, such as Scott Hahn, have put forth the idea that if Adam have fought the devil at this point, he may have died in the conflict defending Eve, his bride, against corruption. But being without sin, and being righteous by the exercise of faith in God, he would have been resurrected to a higher glory than what he knew. Death could not have held Adam in its grip if Adam was without sin.

Since this is what happened to Christ, the one who was fully man, made like Adam without human male intervention, it is not a great stretch to consider this possible. The first Adam was called upon to face death for his bride and failed at it. The Last Adam faced death for His Bride, the Church, and succeeded. Always run the type/antitype parallels in scripture to understand properly themes which are not drawn out word for word.

Let us take this type/antitype and let us imagine a different conclusion to the original temptation in the Garden. Adam resists, quoting to the wicked one the very words of his Father: *"But of the tree of the knowledge of good and evil, thou shalt not eat of it"* This is what Christ did in the desert where He was driven

---

33

Rom 4:13 For the promise, that he should be the heir of the world, was not to Abraham, or to his seed, through the law, but through the righteousness of faith.

after His baptism. He quoted the words of His Father. As perfect man our Lord as the Last Adam succeeded for mankind where Adam failed. Do you see the parallel?

Adam now faces something which he has not prior to this moment. He is tempted and must exercise faith in his Father. Prior to this, everything was perfect. In this second, at this declaration to the wicked one of his faith in his Father, Adam grows in true, intrinsic righteousness. He is no longer merely innocent. He has met evil head on and by his expression of faith, he becomes righteous and grows in righteousness.

Satan attacks and a great struggle ensues. Adam is killed. The wicked one, thinking he has won and defeated the purpose of God, leaves gloating over his easy victory. But righteous Adam is not permitted to suffer corruption. There is no sin in him which is able to drag him into death. Indeed, death cannot hold him. He is raised from this temporary state of physical death and shining in the glory of righteousness, is now given a new title: high priest of God.

His first duty: redemption of his wife, who lies sobbing, terribly changed by her sin, and in need of redemption. Adam calls out to her in love, a love which cannot be quenched by the stain of her disobedience. She approaches with fear and trembling, for her eyes have been opened to see things which she wishes she had never seen. Oh, if only she had listened to God and not that wretched serpent! Kneeling before her earthly lord, she awaits, fearful and unsure of what will happen next.

But then a marvelous thing happens. Adam wipes from his forehead some of the blood which still lays there fresh from his victory over evil. Placing it upon Eve, he offers prayers of intercession to his Father, renewing his covenant family vows and asking his death to be the means of forgiving Eve's transgression. He is still the head of the earthly family. He has not given up his authority because he did not transgress the covenant. And now, because of his faith in God, expressed in an act of resistance to sin, he has been advanced in

40

glory and given new responsibility.

The possibility of sin will always be present. The opportunity to distrust God and fall into sin will always be with the human family. But the Father now has a new answer for sin, a high priest who will mediate between the sinner and God. He will apply the blood of faith and obedience, which was shed in his battle with the wicked one, to Eve and to any of the generations of their children who come to him in their sin. As long as Adam remained untouched by sin himself, remaining the covenant head of the family, he would be able to perform the function of priesthood between God and mankind. All of Adam's children, generation after generation of them, will be able to stand before this priest and have him pronounce forgiveness and restoration over them. Untouched by sin, Adam would be both priest and high priest of the family of mankind. [34]

This is how I came to understand the reason for Adam's temptation. Do you find this a far stretch? Why? Is Christ not called The Last Adam? [35] Can you not see in the story I have told an exact parallel between what Adam *could have done and become* and what Jesus the Christ actually did do as perfect man? Jesus battled temptation from the devil with the commandment of God. Jesus died for His Bride, the Church. Jesus died so that all mankind could be saved. Jesus exists as our Great High Priest, interceding for the Church as the high priest of the OT interceded for God's people.

We know this did not happen. Adam and Eve are driven out of the Garden and mankind multiplies on the face of the earth. In a short span of time,

---

[34]

A priest mediates between God and man for personal sins. The high priest of God intercedes for the whole community of God. Very important difference, and one in which Protestants make a drastic mistake when they conflate the two, saying that there is no need for priests because Christ is our Great High Priest.

[35] 1 Corinthians 15:45

the wickedness of man becomes so great that God grieves [36] over His creation of man and sends a flood to destroy mankind. Yet even now, there will not be a complete destruction of mankind. God will start over with one whom He finds to be righteous.

Noah is righteous and finds grace in the sight of the Lord. Noah and his family are placed in an ark, constructed by Noah at God's command. The whole earth is cleansed of the wickedness of mankind and man begins again. God states He will establish His covenant with Noah. The human family has a chance to be redeemed. There is, I believe, an opportunity to return to the Garden.

But this is not to be. Noah has inherited the same disease which plagued his forefathers, the disease of a nature tainted by sin. You may wonder why I use the term disease in discussing the fall of man. This is the same philosophical construct the Early Fathers of the Church used. They saw man's nature as being diseased by sin, and they called the Eucharist the medicine of immortality. It is not a breaking of law, it is the destruction of our whole nature by an alien influence. It makes us sick so that we cannot act as we should in response to God's love.

Not long after the ark lands on dry ground Noah sins, showing his nature is corrupted by the disease of sin, as has been the nature of every man before him. A new covenant for the family of man cannot be established upon him. He is not to be the last Adam of the human race, the one who redeems everything.

The great heartbeat of mankind is family. You can see this in every culture and every person. There is no culture on earth, no matter how remote and pagan which is not set up in some form of family. While we in America have lost the concept of the village family, in many of the so-called under developed nations, the idea of the tribal community, the large family consisting of many small families, is still quite alive. I remember hearing on TV one morning a

---

[36] Genesis 6:6

woman from Africa describing how in her village, all the members knew all the children and took responsibility for all of them, watching out for both their safety as well as their proper behavior in the society. I found myself thinking of what a wonderful concept it is for the whole village to act as one loving and concerned family, and how bankrupt we are in America by having lost this. In America we have promoted the concept of autonomy and supposed personal freedom over the common good of all and the common care of all by all. The foundation of this attitude is the "me and Jesus" idea of salvation posited by Calvinism. Evangelicalism is not communal and does not understand salvation as membership in family. Salvation in covenant is always part of being part of the covenant group.

The desire to have a family and be part of it is in the heart of each man and woman. We are beings who are made for communion with others, especially those of our own blood. This desire drives adopted children many times to try to connect with their biological fathers and mothers. Family is flesh of flesh, and until this connection is made, many adopted people sense a emptiness in their lives. Even without this, when people are thrown into small groups, such as survivors of a disaster, there often emerges a type of family bonding. On television I have seen groups of homeless children on the streets of major cities describe themselves as a family. They even will have a leader who looks out for the welfare of the group and issues orders for the well being of this family unit.

Family is a unifying source. Stories have come forward from the horrors of war in which enemies, when thrown together, found a common bond in sharing pictures of wives and children. Their theologies, cultures, practices, and political beliefs may have been 180 degrees apart, and have brought them to the brink of killing each other, but once disarmed, a common ground of mercy and sympathy was love and concern for their families.

From where comes this amazing world wide phenomenon, known to every culture and every nation? I believe this can be no less than the image of

God which still resides in us, however terribly marred by sin. In establishing family units, in the desire to marry and have a family, in the desire for unity with others, we are a type and shadow, however imperfectly, the covenant family which is the Godhead of Father, Son, and Holy Spirit. Thus we continue to bear within us the image of God and live it out by our actions.

God, in the beginning, created a world which reflected His unity in covenant. He created a son and placed him in the Garden with the express purpose of bearing His image, carrying His authority, and becoming like Him. His plan was to have a family of human beings who would be like Him in every way but His essence. Their unity in love would be a shadow and type of the unity in love of the Trinity.

Since the Fall, the heartbeat and longing of the human race has been for this fractured family be restored, and the One who is the Last Adam would return to set up His eternal kingdom family here on earth. Interestingly, history is filled with cultures and religions which have their crucified messiah. Some of this lore precedes Christ by thousands of years, testifying to a common knowledge which filled world – the promise of a coming Savior who would redeem the Garden family and establish the kingdom here on earth. This lore began through oral tradition first started by Adam and Eve and passed down from generation to generation. Culture after culture may have distorted it, but the central truth remained – a promised Redeemer would come one day. One who would be son of a woman, redeem mankind, and restore all things. This is why in the lore of pagan religions we can find the theme of a woman bearing a son who is in some way a redeemer. Evangelicals claim that the Catholic religion is based on following these pagan religions, such as the story of Tammuz and Nimrod, but it is actually that the pagan religions are false copy of the true Redeemer yet to come. It is a family promise which was specifically delivered through the Jewish nation to the Church, which in turn administers it to all mankind as the Gospel goes forth from Jerusalem to all the nations of the earth. From Noah, we again see God dealing with a family on earth. Once again, God chooses a man to be the head of His earthly family. This time, the promises extend far into the future. Abraham is promised that his seed (children, offspring) shall be as innumerable as the stars of the heaven. [37] Note the familial nature of the blessing of God. The blessing does not just come upon Abraham. The promise of blessing is to him *and* generation after generation of his offspring.

Genesis 15 shows us the organization of the covenant family on earth. Opposing the pagan tribes with their false gods and demonic worship, God establishes a specific family on earth as the place of salvation from sin, membership in the family of God, and inheritors of eternal life with Him in His covenant relationship of Trinity.

Those who misunderstand the covenant of God claim there are seven (or eleven or thirteen or nineteen, depending on which teacher you follow) different covenants which are made with God. This is erroneous. It is one covenant, the Trinitarian covenant of the eternal God. Each "new covenant" is in reality just a deeper revelation of the one and only covenant, giving further information about God's dealing with mankind through His covenant. The New Covenant of Christ Jesus is the final and completed revelation to mankind. We now have, in Christ Jesus, all we need to know and will know about covenant this side of the grave. The covenant with Adam had one family rule: don't eat of the tree of the knowledge of good and evil. This was the test of Adam's love. Without this test, Adam would have had no exercise of his will and no opportunity for obedience in love. I believe if Adam had obeyed, the revelation of the covenant would have deepened for him. He may not have known he had the potential to be ruler of the cosmos, a subordinate king under the great kingship of God the Father. This state of subordinate kingship is known as a Suzerainty Kingship. The earthly analogy of God as King is found in the Suzerainty kings of the Middle East. Ray Sutton

---

[37] **Genesis 15:5**

and other Reformed writers have written extensively about Suzerainty covenants, which are political covenants and should not be confused with the covenant of salvation, which is a family covenant. Unfortunately, in his book, Sutton superimposes the political covenants of the Suzerain kings over the salvific family covenant of God, thereby making the covenant of God a bare political contract of kingship instead of a family relationship. The principles are correct, the application is all wrong.

There are principles in the marital and familial covenants which parallel the Suzerainty Treaty Covenant. Suzerainty occurs where a region or people is a tributary to a more powerful entity which controls its foreign affairs while allowing the tributary vassal state some limited domestic autonomy. The problem with making the eternal covenant to be a Suzerainty covenant is that it takes an analogy from earth, which is based on two strangers making a treaty, and treats the family relationship as if it follows that pattern. In a Suzerain kingship, two unrelated strangers approach each other from a position of suspicion rather than familial love. The Suzerainty treaty is a contract made from a position of self-interest by both parties.

Now take the same idea of kingship (God the Father) and apply it to loving sons (mankind) and you can see that while there is the respect of God as ever greater than us, the relationship of familial love, even in rulership over Creation, will to be vastly different than that of two entirely unrelated men. Had Adam not fallen, he would have matured into kingship over Creation, with God the Father as the Great Suzerain of the universe. But the relationship would still have been that of the Father as King and Adam the son as lesser king, in a family of unitive love, rather than of two potential combatants seeking to avoid war by making a mutually beneficial contract.

In Abraham, God begins to establish His family on earth. This family is called the church. The word for church in Greek is ἐκκλησα (ekklēsia). In Hebrew it is לְהָק (qāhēl). Both words mean "congregation," "gathering," or "assembly." So the Church is the assembly of those who have been covenanted to God under the blood terms by which covenant is made with God. The purpose of this organized family after the fall is to provide a nation of priests who will represent Creation to God, offering pleasing sacrifices to Him, and be the congregation into which the Messiah will enter, offering Himself as the Last Adam and covenant head over mankind.

With King David, the covenant is further enlarged, revealing one of Abraham's sons (David) being told that his son will sit as ruler over all Creation. It was because of this promise we hear Bartimaeus call out: "Jesus, Son of David, have mercy on me!" He recognized in Jesus the One who was the promised son of David, the One who would sit on the throne of his father, David, and rule forever. In Christ, the covenant is made new, fulfilled, and brought into full revelation to mankind. The covenant body, the qāhēl of Abraham, Moses, David, and Jesus, is the family of God on earth. If the nation of Israel had not killed Christ and thereby destroyed the covenant between them and God, they would be that congregation, the family of God on earth.

What is the restored family of God today? Is it some ethereal, invisible Church which consists of only true believers? That is a popular belief, but I see no warrant for that idea in the Bible. When the congregation of God was discussed, it was always speaking about a visible, physical body on earth with a distinct hierarchical structure and certain places where the worship of God took place. When the writer of Hebrews 2:12 quoted Psalm 22:22, he was speaking of the visible assembly of God's family. When Jesus says, in Matthew 18: 17 to bring disputes to the Church and tell them to the Church, there is no idea there of an invisible body. I believe pride lies behind the refusal of Protestants to see there is but one Church on earth, the same pride which submits to no one or no thing except their own understanding of the Bible.

When the Prodigal Son insulted his father and left the household, was he an active and authorative part of the family? No. He separated himself from the covenant relationship he had with his father. When he came to his senses, he realized what he had given up and returned to be made a servant. This attitude of repentance, recognized by his father, moved his father to restore their covenant relationship. There is powerful symbolism in the articles which are brought out for the Prodigal. The robe, the ring, and the sandals are all symbols of complete restoration of sonship and household authority. He will not be treated as a field slave. He is once again son, with all privileges, and the unity of relationship is fully restored. He has ended his separation by coming to his senses, admitting his insane guilt, and seeking forgiveness and restoration.

This is what the Roman Catholic church must do to be restored to the covenant unity and fellowship of the Church. Rome is not the Church. The Church in the early centuries of Christianity was a family of five patriarchs [38] under the covenant headship of the Last Adam – Christ. Rome has abrogated to itself an authority which it does not have. [39]

When the Frankish bishops overtook Rome and installed the Filioque Clause into the Creed, violating the Seventh Canon of the Third Ecumenical Council, [40] which pronounces an anathema upon anyone changing the Creed, they severed themselves from the unity of the Church. In a sad demonstration of pride and arrogance, this severance was furthered in 1054 AD when the papal legate of Rome, Cardinal Humberto, slapped a bull of excommunication on the altar of the Hagia Sophia during the Divine Liturgy.

---

[38] Rome, Antioch, Alexandria, Constantinople and Jerusalem.

[39] See my information on the misinterpretation of Matthew 16 in the last chapter of this book

[40] Canon VII: These things having been read aloud, the holy Council then decreed that no one should be permitted to offer any different belief or faith, or in any case to write or compose any other, than the one defined by the Holy Fathers who convened in the city of Nicaea, with Holy Spirit.

48

From there, further events have come to show that the ecclesial body at Rome has gone into the far country of strange doctrines and dogmas not known by the early church. Indeed, the faith that the Roman church espouses now is not the faith once delivered to the saints.[41] Dogmatic inventions such as the Immaculate Conception, Indulgences, Purgatory, the Treasury of Merit, Papal Infallibility, Papal Supremacy, and of course, the Filioque, were created without the meeting of an ecumenical council. Until they are discarded, there can be no unity in error, no commonality of mind, no fellowship. The Roman Catholics who practice them are beloved sons of the Father and as baptized ones, part of the covenant, but are in the far country of error. We long for them to come home.

There is one other thing about Adam which is unique to him alone – he was created into covenant. We, as Christians, are *adopted* sons and daughters. As such, we *choose* whether or not to enter into the family covenant. A biblical picture of this would be the marriage feast of Matthew 22. Those who wish to become part of this New Covenant and the kingship of our Last Adam, come to Him through faith and enter into unity by baptism. In doing so, we make an oath (sacramentum) by which we bind ourselves to fidelity to the rules of the kingdom. This is also why marriage is a Sacrament, for it is a covenant which is made with oaths (sacramentum) in love between the betrothed.

Adam was created into the covenant which already existed as part of the heavenly family, the eternal covenant. In any culture, the son born into the family is a part of the family covenant, under the headship of the father, the love and help of the mother, and is bound by birth to keep the family rules. It is a covenant of blood, made by the shedding of the mother's blood in birth (all covenants are blood oaths and everywhere covenant with God is made you will in some manner

---

[41] Jude 1:3 Beloved, when I gave all diligence to write unto you of the common salvation, it was needful for me to write unto you, and exhort you that ye should earnestly contend for the faith which was once delivered unto the saints.

find blood or reference to blood). The wise father explains to the child as he is growing up what is expected of him as heir and family member. Violation of these family standards results in familial discord. A serious enough violation results in losing the family inheritance.

I believe Christ, as man in both nature and physical existence, picked up right where Adam failed. It was no accident that immediately after His baptism, which began His ministry on earth, Christ was driven out into the desert to take up the fallen banner of temptation which Adam had dropped. He goes right to the point where the first Adam failed, temptation by the Evil One.

The purpose of the redemption then, was not just so that individual sinners would come to God, but that the whole human family, separated by sin, would be restored as the covenant family of the heavenly Father. As all were lost in Adam, separated from God by the gulf of sin his disobedience created, so now is all mankind reunited to God by the obedience of the Last Adam.

Ro 5:18 Therefore as by the offence of one judgment came upon all men to condemnation; even so by the righteousness of one the free gift came upon all men unto justification of life. 19 For as by one man's disobedience many were made sinners, so by the obedience of one shall many be made righteous.

I believe this is the state of the world today. Mankind is restored to the Father. Because of this restoration in Christ, it is the responsibility of every man and woman to seek separation from Adam through the waters of baptism and enter into covenant with Christ. Through this union with Christ all may enjoy the full benefits of His restoration of the human family and its covenant with the Father. Salvation is being part of the covenant/family relationship with God. The family is the Church.

SUMMARY

Mankind is a family, created by the love/union of the Trinity. Love is life-giving and creating. Although created as unique individuals, we are part of a greater whole, descendants of one man. Families are covenant relationships. They have heads (fathers) and helpmeets (mothers). There are offspring who grow up to be fathers and mothers. Our family on earth has a name and a structure. The family is the congregation, or Church In this family are rules which are structures of love by which we might live in peace and harmony with each other. In the Church is a way to give our love to our Father by offering Him our praise, worship, and the Sacrifice most pleasing to Him, the Eucharist.

RESTORING OUR MOTHER

One commonality between Orthodoxy and Catholicism from the very first centuries of the Church is the love and honor we give to Mary. In Orthodoxy, we refer to her as the Theotokos, the "God-bearer." For Protestants, the titles given to the Blessed Virgin, the honor and love shown to her, create no small scandal. And the titles that are given to her! Horrors!

How do we justify such actions? It is sad that many Orthodox and Catholic lay people cannot give a satisfactory answer to Protestant objections. Objections are met with either platitudes or quiet confusion. This lack of understanding in every Catholic layperson I ever met until a few years ago was the basis of my thinking that the Catholic faith was a religion for the simple minded who had allowed themselves to be fooled by priests. Yet the answer is, like all apostolic dogmas, found in a proper understanding of our covenant family.

What would you say of a man who was given a wrecked car and told to restore it to the same condition as it was before the wreck, only to return to you half-done? You certainly wouldn't think very much of his workmanship and you would probably warn your friends and co-workers to avoid his shop at all costs. A job half-done is a job not done at all.

Yet this is exactly what Protestantism teaches about the Redemption of our Lord in denying the Queenship of our Lady and Her right to our honor. This problem comes from the highly individualized view of salvation extant in Protestantism. Everything is viewed from the aspect of "what's in this for me?" instead of the overview of God's salvific work in all of Creation. It is a very truncated and narrow view of God's redemptive work.

What exactly was lost in the Garden? Were a couple of vassal slaves tossed out on their ear to beg forgiveness and hope they could get back in? Oh, no! The damage was far more deep and pervasive than that. Remember, Adam was created as son of the Great King. Therefore, the first thing that was lost was his potential rulership one day as king of Creation. That is what sons of kings do – they mature into kings themselves one day, and in a large kingdom, they will take rule themselves as subordinate kings to their father. Adam forfeited this, along with his priesthood and the future possibility of being the great high priest over Creation to intercede for any of his posterity who would sin.

His nature was corrupted, and that corruption was handed down to every generation which came from his loins. Because of this corruption, Adam and Eve lost their unity with God and fell in to a state of separation from Him called death. This separation came because Adam's corrupted nature could not share in God's divine nature. The divine nature of self-donative love would have found itself incompatible with mankind's corrupted sin nature, which seeks only its own pleasure and good.

He lost covenant headship over the family of God on earth which is mankind. In losing the authority of covenant headship, his position of fatherhood over mankind was forfeit, for the appellation of father describes one who is a covenant head over a covenant unit called the family. And likewise, his wife lost her position of covenant motherhood. It is not just Adam who is affected. This was a disaster on many levels!

What did Jesus accomplish as perfect Man? As the Last Adam, He regained kingship and rules now as King over all Creation. As man He is the Great High Priest in the tabernacle made without hands in the heavenlies. As man He perfects man's nature in His body, being totally obedient to His Father and then performing for us the greatest act of self-donative love ever seen in the cosmos. The Creator of all allows those whom He created to spit upon Him, mock Him, scourge and beat Him, and send Him to death on a cruel cross. And He does this so that the very men who do it to Him can be saved from the evil that drives them to do such a heinous act. It is the ultimate display of the nature of God – cruciform, self-giving love for the good of the other.

The Last Adam does what first Adam failed to do. The first Adam, through his sin, forfeits the possibility of becoming everything that the Last Adam becomes. In Christ Jesus, every effect of the fall is reversed and all that mankind possesses in the Garden is restored. Rev. Ralph Smith, a Reformed writer, states the same thing:

"It is what salvation is all about because salvation is restoration – not merely restoration to the original state in Eden but to the attainment of the goal of Eden." [42]

This is an amazing statement, but Rev. Smith has not followed his thinking to the logical outcome. There was another person in the Garden. The covenant helpmeet. What of her? If Eve is not restored in full, then the work of God's redemptive plan is only half done. Everything must be restored completely to the condition that it was in before the Fall. Before the Fall, there was a human

---

[42] **Rev. Ralph Allen Smith | Eternal Covenant-How The Trinity Reshapes Covenant Theology, Page 59 | Canon Press | 2003**

mother of all with a nature uncorrupted by sin and the possibility of becoming a queen next to her king husband. If God restored Adam as male human being, then in order to *fully restore* that which He created in the Garden, He must also restore Eve in the person of a female human being. To leave Eve out of the equation would be to leave the redemptive work of the Father incomplete. There would be no regeneration. Certainly the Early Church Fathers understood this, for they referred to Mary as the New Eve.

Let's look at some of the parallels between Eve and Mary, beginning with their creation as human beings.

Eve was created by the work of God in splitting open Adam's side. The Theotokos was created in the same way, by the splitting open of the side of the Last Adam. Both were created sinless. There was no need for an "Immaculate Conception" because Augustine's idea of all people bearing the guilt of Adam's sin does not exist. All children are born innocent. In order to sin, you must have three things which a baby cannot have: knowledge of good and evil, choice to do evil, commission of that evil. A baby can do none of this. The only thing that human beings experience from Adam's sin is the death which is the consequence of Adam's disobedience. That comes to us all.

Eve was the wife of a prince. As son of the Great King, Adam had the potential of kingship and rulership, which means that Eve would have become a queen to rule with him.

Building on the biblical image of Christ as the Last Adam, early Christians spoke of the New Eve, a feminine cooperator with Jesus in the economy of the redemption. Second century writers Saints Justin Martyr and Irenaeus of Lyons perceived Mary as this second Eve, who undid the sin of the first one:

"Christ became man by the Virgin that the disobedience which issued from the serpent might be destroyed in the same way it originated. Eve was still

an undefiled virgin when she conceived the word of the serpent and brought forth disobedience and death. But the Virgin received faith and joy, at the announcement of the angel Gabriel...and she replied, "Be it done to me according to your word". So through the mediation of the Virgin he came into the world, through whom God would crush the serpent and those angels and men like him, who delivers from death those who turn from their evil ways and believe in him." [43]

"The seduction of a fallen angel drew Eve, a virgin espoused to a man, while the glad tidings of the holy angel drew Mary, a Virgin already espoused, to begin the plan which would dissolve the bonds of that first snare...For as the former was led astray by the word of an angel, so that she fled from God when she had disobeyed his word, so did the latter, by an angelic communication, receive the glad tidings that she should bear God, and obeyed his word. If the former disobeyed God, the latter obeyed, so that the Virgin Mary might become the advocate of the virgin Eve. Thus, as the human race fell into bondage to death by means of a virgin, so it is rescued by a virgin; virginal disobedience is balanced in the opposite scale by virginal obedience." [44]

In like manner, the Blessed Virgin, as the new Eve to the Last Adam, is the helpmeet. She bears rulership with Him, not of herself intrinsically, but of God, in the same way that Adam and Eve would have borne the authority of God had they not fallen. When titles such as Intercessor, Mediator, and other appellations which drive Protestants just wild, are given to her, they are given because she, as helpmeet, equally bears that authority that her *human son,* the Last Adam, has been given in heaven.

---

[43] **Justin Martyr | Dialogue with Trypho | ch.100.**

[44] **Irenaeus of Lyons | Against Heresies III:22:4.**

Remember, it is a *man* who rules in heaven. Yes, a special man who is, in a mystery, both human and divine, two natures not comingled, yet existing in one person. A man and a woman, *a human king and queen in heaven,* now rule in covenant headship over the human family. This was exactly what God had planned for Adam and Eve and exactly what He restored in Jesus and the Virgin Mary, Kingship and Queenship over the created world.

Unfortunately, this is what I missed when I left Protestantism for the Byzantine Catholic Church, a church in communion with the errors of Rome. Had I put more thought into it, I would have realized that only the Last Adam could replace the first Adam. Adam, a man, was covenant head to all mankind and over all creation. Only the man, Christ Jesus, fills that position perfectly. To say that the pope is the head of the Church is to usurp that position which rightly belongs to Christ. Furthermore, there is no document anywhere in which the Bishop of Rome is given the important covenant title The Last Adam.

Not only are the positions and authority of king and queen redeemed in Jesus and Mary, but we now have father and mother of us all once again to watch over us. This is another of those lost titles which Adam and Eve forfeited by the Fall. Think of it this way. Imagine the world without the fall. Imagine that King Adam and Queen Eve are still on earth, still reigning over creation in the splendor of their fully formed imaging of God. As human beings they are creatures who are as beautiful and splendid as Christ was on the Mount of Transfiguration. The shekinah glory of God covers them as it did Moses when he descended from Mount Sinai. Their rule extends to not only this earth, but to planets which have been formed from divine fiat of the Godhead. Perhaps there are children of men on these planets and they bear similar rule over the creation there They would have grown in holiness and righteousness to such a degree that they would be able to hear and answer the thoughts and requests of all their children on earth from where ever on earth they would be.

Do you find this hard to believe? Why?

Matthew 12:25 And Jesus _knew their thoughts_, and said unto them, Every kingdom divided against itself is brought to desolation; and every city or house divided against itself shall not stand:

Luke 6:8 But he _knew their thoughts_, and said to the man which had the withered hand, Rise up, and stand forth in the midst. And he arose and stood forth.

Remember, as man, our Lord Jesus is the Last Adam. This indicates that all that He has as a fully developed man, Adam could have had. Eve would have shared in these attributes of the divine nature as his helpmeet. And all of their children could have also grown into this. Ultimately, as believers, this what we look forward to as gods/children of the King. We have even seen this in the lives of the saints who had abilities such as the reading of souls and bilocation.

From where ever we would be on the planet, we could think in silent prayer our requests to them. As our father and mother, they would be worthy of praise. In fact, we would be expected to give it to them:

Ex 20:12 Honour thy father and thy mother: that thy days may be long upon the land which the LORD thy God giveth thee.

"Now wait a minute!" I hear someone say. _"Adam is not my father. I know who my father is and it is not Adam!"_

But the Bible teaches us differently. Look, for instance, at what Jesus says to the Jews:

Joh 8:56 _Your father_ Abraham rejoiced to see my day: and he saw it, and was glad.

58

Jesus tells the Jews thousands of years separated from Abraham that he is their father. Why? Because it was from his seed that the entire lineage of the Jews sprang forth. He is truly the father of the Jewish nation, for his blood flows in the veins of every Jewish person. Even more true then is the fact that Adam is the father of us all, for from him came the whole human race.

Just as Eve was called the mother of all living, so now is the Virgin Mary the Mother of all who are truly alive in Christ and share in His divine life. How much more then, for the Christian, should he refer to God as His Father, and the Virgin Mary *as his Mother*, for without the grace of God and the willingness of Mary to submit to God's will, we would still be in a state of separation from God and slavery to sin. This is why we treat her with respect and give her our supplications. She is the New Eve indeed.

Imagine if you will, Earth in a state of splendor without the fall. You come to me one day and say *"I have taken time off from my duties and am going to go see our ruler, Queen Eve, to pay her my respects."*

Would I chide you and say, *"How dare you call her the ruler! Adam alone is the ruler over this earth! She is but his helpmeet and a mere creation of God!"*

Not likely, if you have understood the principle of unity I have set out in earlier paragraphs. Adam and Eve would be <u>one flesh and one mind</u>. As such, to call one by the title ruler is to acknowledge and honor the other one who makes up the whole. Separation of rulership came only after the fall. And even then, Eve still retained a position higher than the children who would come from her womb. Thus the commandment says not "Honor thy father . . ." but instead "Honor thy father and thy mother." Even in a subordinate position to Adam, Eve still bears in his authority a place of dignity and honor. In each normal human family (and God knows there are some weird and abnormal ones out there) the father treats disrespect of the mother as disrespect of himself and his own authority. In a properly functional family, the mother represents the father, therefore, disrespect to her is disrespect to the one who has given her the authority and in whose name she ultimately speaks. Swift and serious punishment is the consequence for a child who insults his father by disrespect to his mother.

Does that sound alien to you, like something from a fairy tale? That shows you then how far out of touch we have become with the principles of the covenant family which God established to be the norm. A wife ordering a husband around, emotionally or sexually blackmailing him to get her way, ought to be an open scandal.

If the first Adam was still on earth in his glorified state, it would be no sin to ask favor of him and to glorify him. Neither would it be wrong to approach Eve and request her intercession. Since Adam and Eve have been covenantally restructured in Jesus and Mary, then we do no sin to honor them in this manner.

This understanding of the plan of God in the Garden covenant for His family makes the honor we bestow upon Mary to be a simple continuation of that which was interrupted in the Garden. By her obedience to God, the Virgin Mary receives that which Eve forfeited. The honor of her children, the blessings of obedience, including Her reign in heaven, and the sharing of the authority given to the Last Adam, reigning and ruling with Him in perfect unity of will, all belong to the Blessed Virgin. In this lavish praise, let me remind you once again that just as Adam and Eve would have had perfect unity of will in the Garden if there had been no Fall, so does the Blessed Virgin do nothing but the divine will of Her Son, Who, in turn, said of Himself as man.

John 5: 19 "Then answered Jesus and said unto them, Verily, verily, I say unto you, The Son can do nothing of himself, but what he seeth the Father do: for what things soever he doeth, these also doeth the Son likewise."

When Jesus thus spoke, saying that He could do nothing of Himself, He was speaking as the perfect *man*. Remember that Christ is both divine and human. Two natures in one person. Therefore, we know that as a perfect and sinless human being, the replacement for Eve, the Blessed Virgin also acts only in obedience to and conformity with the divine will of God. In honoring the Virgin, in asking Her intercession for us, we do not treat Her as some sort of extra god or divine person who, like the Greek gods of mythology, engaged in war among themselves. She will only pray the will of God for us.

As I began to understand this connection between Eve and Mary, I found other information from the scriptures which is never spoken of in Protestantism. I find it fascinating to realize that while Protestants are very quick to recognize the types of Christ in the OT, eagerly pointing to David as a type of Christ, or the ram which Abraham found and substituted for his son as a picture of Christ's substitute for sinners, it seems they go absolutely blind when it comes to Marian typology in OT.

One of the ones which is most interesting is that of the Ark of the Covenant. The Ark contained three things: the rod of Jesse which bloomed, the Word of God, and the manna from heaven. Did Mary also contain in her body these same three things? Is not Jesus the son of Jesse which bloomed for our salvation? Is He not the living bread come down from heaven? He is the living Word. All of this points to Mary as the Ark of the New Covenant.

Which, in turn, points directly to Her ever-virginity. No man was allowed to touch the Ark. The Ark was set apart for a special use unto God. No profane use could be made of it.

In keeping with the familial understanding of God's covenant dealings, another typology is of Mary as spouse of the Holy Spirit. This is not something new which I have come up with either. The writings of the Early Fathers make it abundantly clear that they regarded the placing of the Divine Word within Her womb as a spousal action by the Holy Spirit.

"(The Holy Spirit) Who is so singularly with Mary is the Lord Whose most beautiful spouse Mary is...Behold, a beautiful spouse, beautiful in justice, and in the judgment of her looks, beautiful in compassion and in mercy in the regard of her neighbors, and beautiful in faith in the sight of God" [45]

Please read the next section carefully and thoughtfully. It is important to understand that *in no way are we attributing a physical, sexual union to Mary and the Holy Spirit.*

Spouse of the Holy Spirit

This title has caught on more strongly than the first two. It is a well-established part of the common series of Marian titles Daughter of God the Father, Mother of God the Son, Spouse of God the Holy Spirit

The Christian poet Prudentius (348-c.405) first used this image in relation to the Annunciation: "The unwed Virgin espoused the Spirit." The list of Christians who called Mary the Spouse of the Spirit is impressive: Saints Anselm of Canterbury, Francis of Assisi, Bonaventure, Lawrence of Brindisi, Louis Marie de Montfort and Maximilian Kolbe, to name a few. Various modern popes have used or alluded to it, including Leo XII, Pius XII and Paul VI.

In his encyclical, *Marialis Cultus*, Pope Paul VI wrote that early Christians coined the title Spouse of the Holy Spirit because they saw in the relationship between Mary and the Spirit "an aspect redolent of marriage" Exactly what is that "aspect"?

Some may point to the fact that Mary conceived Jesus by the power of the Spirit as indicating a "marital" relationship. Yet we must not take this too far,

---

[45] Bonaventure, quoted in Virgin Wholly Marvelous: Praises of Our Lady by the Popes, Councils, Saints and Doctors of the Church |, Ed. David Supple (Still River, MA: Ravengate, 1981): 37.

for it could lead to the belief that the Holy Spirit is the "father" of Jesus in the Incarnation. Though Mary did conceive Jesus by the power of the Spirit, the latter did not play a parental role in the conception. A parent contributes his or her own substance to the child. Thus the First Divine Person is Christ's Eternal Father Who generates the Word from His own nature, and Mary is truly His earthly Mother who gave Him His Humanity. But the Spirit contributes nothing to Jesus at His conception, and so is in no sense His Father. [46]

Saint Maximillian Kolbe presents us with a more profound solution:

The union brought about by married love is the most intimate of all. In a much more precise, more interior, more essential manner, the Holy Spirit lives in the soul of the Immaculata, in the very depths of her being.

He goes on to say that the relationship between the Spirit of God and the Theotokos is redolent of a marriage in the following ways:

♦ As a husband and wife become "one flesh" in marriage (Genesis 2:24) yet remain distinct persons, so Mary and the Spirit are two distinct persons who share a deep spiritual union.

♦ As human spouses cooperate in giving life to their children, so, analogously, the Spirit and Mary "cooperate" in communicating spiritual life to us.

Interestingly, these two things actually reflect the "unitive and procreative" aspects of human conjugal love. Now the union between Mary and the Third Divine Person is **spiritual, not at all sexual, for the Holy Spirit is pure Spirit like the Father, and so could not possibly have a physical relationship with Mary.**

What was stated above regarding the titles Wife of the Father and Bride

---

[46]   Augustine, Enchiridion XL | Saint Thomas Aquinas, Summa Theologica | pt. III q.32 art.3.

of Christ applies equally to Spouse of the Holy Spirit. None of these three titles indicate a physical or sexual relationship between God and Mary. Rather, all have a deeper, spiritual significance which transcends the flesh. [47]

I would urge any Protestant who is at this moment horrified to read what I have written to go to the website I have posted in the footnotes and do a thorough read of the entire article. Reading this article will make it abundantly clear that while Mary has been through the centuries regarded as the Spouse of the Holy Trinity, it is in a *spiritual sense only* that this is regarded.

However, in keeping with this understanding of the deep, intimate union of spouses, no man allows another man to touch in intimacy the spouse he has taken to himself. How much more then was Mary set aside from the joys of physical intimacy to a profoundly higher joy – deep intimacy with God. It is the same deep intimacy we shall enjoy with Him forever as His Bride. The earthly, sexual aspect of conjugal love only points, very poorly, to a union in heaven which is light years beyond the physical here on earth in intimacy and love.

SUMMARY

Every family has a father and mother, a covenant head (greater authority) and a covenant helpmeet (lesser authority). Without these two positions, there is no family. Our family was cast out of the Garden and Adam lost his headship authority. Another man, Jesus the Christ, has regained it, being called the Last Adam. To complete the restoration of the Edenic family, there had to be a human female who would compliment the Last Adam. Only the Theotokos qualifies. Because she is Mother over the redeemed human race, we honor and praise her for her obedience to God. Honor is not worship.

---

[47] **The Mystical Rose Catholic Page | MARY, THE BRIDE OF GOD PART 2: CHURCH TEACHING | http://home.earthlink.net/~mysticalrose/bride2.html. While these writings are distinctly Roman Catholic, there are also prayers in Orthodoxy which refer to Mary as the Spouse of God.**

THE LANGUAGE OF
THE FAMILY REDEMPTION

I have tried to show that the relationship of God to mankind is that of family, not vassal slaves. I have attempted to show how Jesus and Mary, in a covenant sense of headship and helpmeet, restore the lost Edenic family of Adam and Eve. Now I wish to show the things I found regarding the Church as the New Covenant family of God which replaced national Israel as the ekklesia of God, the congregation of his people. If the Church is indeed the congregation of God, then Her doctrines must be God's truth for all men to obey.

I think it important to begin with a discussion of the language used in speaking of Christ's salvific work. Improper use of scriptural terms is a cause of much of the misunderstanding between Catholics and Protestants regarding God's redemptive work. The foundational problem I see is that neither Protestants nor Catholics think in terms of covenant. To add to this problem, Protestant exegesis has muddied the soteriological waters by making the words redemption, redeemed, born-again, regeneration, and saved, and all mean eternal life. This is confusing. I think it time to start teaching covenant reality, since we are people of the covenant of God.

REDEMPTION – This is the great plan of God for *all* mankind. The universality of the redemptive work finds its scriptural basis in passages such as 1 John 2: 2; 1 Tim 2: 4 and others which bear out the Redeemer's all-encompassing salvific intention, contrary to the Calvinist notion that the death of Christ was only for the elect. Christ's sacrificial death and glorious resurrection restores the *kosmos* to its proper position in union with the covenant Head Who comes from mankind and Who is perfect man. The family covenant which was broken in the Garden is redeemed. Protestants have a habit of making redemption an individual act. It is not. Redemption is spoken of and understood *corporately* in scripture.

By bearing the title of Last Adam, I find it reasonable to say that Christ died not for all sins of all individuals, but for the sin of Adam, so that in like manner that Adam condemned all his posterity yet within his loins, the redemption of Adam by Christ has the far reaching effect of restoring the covenant of God so that all men are put back into the Garden-standing which they had before Adam's sin. The Fathers of the Church teach that by assuming our nature, Christ changes it. Not individually. In Christ, mankind as a whole is healed and restored to the Father. This is a corporate covenant, made between the Last Adam and the Father for the redemption of the cosmos and all in it. It is different from the individual covenant we must make with Christ through baptism into Him. In another way of thinking, redemption is the creation of salvation for all, but we must each individually enter into it with a personal covenant of salvation.

With the door to the kingdom family thus open, it is for each man to be entered into the redemption which is in the Last Adam. By dint of our fleshly union to him, we are all united to Adam and partake of the ontological effects of his covenant breaking. [48] The Orthodox Church sees these effects as sickness in our very nature, and the redemption of Christ provides a medicine by which we are healed. I believe it is correct to see redemption as the exact reversal of what was lost and how it was lost. As condemnation for mankind as a whole came by our being in Adam, so redemption for mankind as a whole comes from mankind being in the Last Adam.

I have no doubt there will be some who read this and will say this sounds uncomfortably like Universalism, the idea that everyone is going to eventually be saved. While I say that Christ has indeed saved all mankind by redeeming mankind and all creation to God, [49] what I have not discussed is what effect this will have upon individuals. Mankind as a whole has been restored to God in the Person of Christ. The evil one has no more corporate claim upon either Creation or mankind. But the fact that now all have been returned to God does not mean that all will enjoy that relationship forever.

"One could insist, however, that the Sacred Scriptures and the Fathers always speak of God as the Great Judge who will reward those who were obedient to Him and will punish those who were disobedient, in the day of the Great Judgment (II Tim. 4:6-8). How are we to understand this judgment if we are to understand the divine words not in a human but in a divine manner'? What is God's judgment?

God is Truth and Light. God's judgment is nothing else than our coming into contact with truth and light. In the day of the Great Judgment all men will appear naked before this penetrating light of truth. The "books" will be opened. What are these "books"? They are our hearts. Our hearts will be opened by the

---

[48] **Romans 5: 12**

[49] **Romans 5: 18-19**

penetrating light of God, and what is in these hearts will be revealed. If in those hearts there is love for God, those hearts will rejoice seeing God's light. If, on the contrary, there is hatred for God in those hearts, these men will suffer by receiving on their opened hearts this penetrating light of truth which they detested all their life.

So that which will differentiate between one man and another will not be a decision of God, a reward or a punishment from Him, but that which was in each one's heart; what was there during all our life will be revealed in the Day of Judgment. If there is a reward and a punishment in this revelation — and there really is — it does not come from God but from the love or hate which reigns in our heart. Love has bliss in it, hatred has despair, bitterness, grief, affliction, wickedness, agitation, confusion, darkness, and all the other interior conditions which compose hell (I Cor. 4:6).

The Light of Truth, God's Energy, God's grace which will fall on men unhindered by corrupt conditions in the Day of Judgment, will be the same to all men. There will be no distinction whatever. All the difference lies in those who receive, not in Him Who gives. The sun shines on healthy and diseased eyes alike, without any distinction. Healthy eyes enjoy light and because of it see clearly the beauty which surrounds them. Diseased eyes feel pain, they hurt, suffer, and want to hide from this same light which brings such great happiness to those who have healthy eyes.

But alas, there is no longer any possibility of escaping God's light. During this life there was. In the New Creation of the Resurrection, God will be everywhere and in everything. His light and love will embrace all. There will be no place hidden from God, as was the case during our corrupt life in the kingdom of the prince of this world. The devil's kingdom will be despoiled by the Common Resurrection and God will take possession again of His creation. Love will enrobe everything with its sacred Fire which will flow like a river from the throne of God and will irrigate paradise. But this same river of Love — for those who have hate in their hearts — will suffocate and burn.

'For our God is a consuming fire.' One could insist, however, that the Sacred Scriptures and the Fathers always speak of God as the Great Judge who will reward those who were obedient to Him and will punish those who were disobedient, in the day of the Great Judgment (II Tim. 4:6-8). How are we to understand this judgment if we are to understand the divine words not in a human but in a divine manner'? What is God's judgment?

"For our God is a consuming fire", (Heb. 12:29). The very fire which purifies gold, also consumes wood. Precious metals shine in it like the sun, rubbish burns with black smoke. All are in the same fire of Love. Some shine and others become black and dark. In the same furnace steel shines like the sun, whereas clay turns dark and is hardened like stone. The difference is in man, not in God.

The difference is conditioned by the free choice of man, which God respects absolutely. God's judgment is the revelation of the reality which is in man. Heb. 12:29). The very fire which purifies gold, also consumes wood. Precious metals shine in it like the sun, rubbish burns with black smoke. All are in the same fire of Love. Some shine and others become black and dark. In the same furnace steel shines like the sun, whereas clay turns dark and is hardened like stone. The difference is in man, not in God." [50]

Dr. Kalomiros' paper shows us the issue is not with God, for not only has He willed to redeem all mankind, as the scriptures state, but in Christ's work alone He has done just this. The issue is one of individual responsibility to heed the call of God to enter into Christ. It is this affirmative individual response which is called salvation.

---

[50] **THE RIVER OF FIRE by ALEXANDRE KALOMIROS | As presented at the 1980 ORTHODOX CONFERENCE sponsored by St. Nectarios American Orthodox Church. Seattle, WA**

SALVATION – Salvation is defined in Kittle's Theological Dictionary of the New Testament as having either spiritual or physical properties. For instance, one can experience salvation, or being saved by being rescued from raging flood waters. That is salvation. It is personal and individual. It is the state of being rescued from that which would do us great harm or death.

We see salvation as a type in the great exodus of the Jews from Egypt. The redemptive plan was established by God for the whole nation. It was open to all, not only Jews, but the random pagans and Egyptians who, believing upon God in fear of the threatened curses, placed themselves in His covenant by partaking of Passover. This redemptive plan was given through a particular nation. Personal salvation from the curse of God came about by a personal salvific choice to enter God's kingdom, the Jewish nation, and go with them out of the accursed land of Egypt. The way was made open to anyone and all who would leave Egypt. There was no sense of an elect who alone were allowed to leave Egypt, with the rest cursed to remain. It was all about individual choice, and scripture indicates there were Egyptians who decided it was better to be with God's people than to live in the devil's false paradise of Egypt.

This is a picture of our salvation now, the same picture Dr. Kalomiros gives us in his paper. The redemption of all mankind, of all who have ever lived, is accomplished in Christ. Our need is to be entered into the redemptive nation of the Church and thus experience salvation individually.

The deliverance of the Jewish people from Egypt is a wonderful picture of the redemptive plan for all mankind, showing both the universal application of salvation which is good for all, yet the individual responsibility to take action and enter that redemptive work. As children of Adam, we are born slaves of sin, a hard taskmaster who enslaves us all, making our lives a bitter weariness and sorrow. God has raised up a Deliverer and has made available to all mankind the journey out of the Egypt of sin enslaving us. No one will be turned away, no one is not of the elect and therefore cursed from birth.

70

The deliverance came in a way the Israelites would have never imagined, through the parted deep waters of the Red Sea and onto the dry land of freedom on the other side. This is a picture of baptism, in which, according to the Bible, we are indeed saved. Just as real as the physical salvation of the Jews by the parting of the waters of the Red Sea, so real is the spiritual salvation of the soul by the parting of the waters of the baptismal tank as we are submerged into the death of Christ and raised to new life in Him:

Ro 6:3 Know ye not, that so many of us as were baptized into Jesus Christ were baptized into his death? 4 Therefore we are buried with him by baptism into death: that like as Christ was raised up from the dead by the glory of the Father, even so we also should walk in newness of life.

Do you see the type/antitype connection? We are really and truly removed from the condemnation we have by being flesh of Adam's flesh, and are placed in Christ by being entered into Christ. This is exactly what the terms saved and salvation mean. We have been just as rescued by our baptism as the Jews were rescued from the Egyptians. Please use these two words carefully and try not to confuse them in your speech. To speak of what Christ did for the world as salvation brings in confusion. Salvation is our personal application of His redemptive plan to our lives. It is only done once. Just as once through the deep waters of the Red Sea there was no turning back, so in like manner, once a person is adopted into the family by baptism into the covenant of God's grace, there is no becoming an unchristian, even if one falls away. It is, in fact, much worse for those who have known and the truth and then have turned from the oath they took in baptism. Covenant breakers receive the curses of the covenant they have broken.

The worst confusion over God's salvation plan comes from those who ask "Are you saved?" or "Are you born-again?" To these folks, generally

Evangelicals, all three of these words mean to have eternal life. Some will even go so far as to ask if you have eternal life and then proceed to show you that being saved or born again means to have eternal life. It does not. Salvation is the beginning of a life-long journey into our final union with God.

BORN AGAIN – The historic Church teaching in both East and West correctly teaches that we are born-again when we are baptized. This is the understanding from the very first century of the Church. The idea of being born-again by waving one's hand, marching up an aisle, and saying a "sinner's prayer," only goes back to around the 1850's at best, having been introduced by Charles G. Finney. It was said of Mr. Finney that he ruined more people for true Christianity than he ever got saved. Sacramental churches reported for years after a Finney crusade in their towns, the people were spiritually ruined. Let's unpack the words and observe the differences.

Gennaô – to be born. *Anôthen* – from above, from a higher place.

There is no indication of the reception of unending eternal life in this verse. It is a fond Protestant invention. Moreover, there is a complete denial of covenant in the idea of making a decision for Jesus and receiving eternal life as a result.

Born again does not mean eternal life. If we use the family analogy we have been referring to over and over in this book, it means to be born into a family, the family of God. Jesus clarifies in John 3:8 that this means to be born of the Spirit instead of the flesh. We are born from above by the grace of God which makes baptism work. Contrary to Anabaptist insinuation, we do not believe there is some kind of magic to the water. It is the Spirit working through baptism which places us in Christ and thus gives to us new life. It is the Sacrament of covenant making which has replaced circumcision.

Nicodemus' fleshly thinking places him in utter confusion as he asks if one must enter again into his mother's womb to be born again. The Greek word

72

anôthen can also have the secondary meaning of again. No doubt this led to the confusion in Nicodemus' thinking, since he was not thinking in spiritual terms regarding rebirth. He was wondering how to get back into his mother!

Why do we need to be born again?

It is because the death which Adam handed down to his posterity, the entire human race, is not only a covenant position of being dead, of being out of covenant and in a *state of separation* from God, it is also a state of being infected by a sickness which makes us unfit for eternal life. Unlike the Calvinist doctrine of Total Depravity, the reality is that this sickness does not remove the free will of man. It leaves intact the image of God in us in which we are responsible for the decisions we make in this life as moral agents.

Ro 5:12 Wherefore, as by one man sin entered into the world, and death by sin; and so death passed upon all men, for that all have sinned:

The above is a statement not of individual sin, but of corporate sin, coming from Adam's violation of God's covenant. In that sense are all men dead to and separated from God, for by natural birth we all exist in Adam corporately as mankind. We are all organically connected to our father Adam and share in his state of separation, which is death. When Adam was in covenant with God he was in relationship with the One who is life. In the Garden, God gave Adam the terms of the covenant family. By keeping these rules, Adam would stay in a love/union with his Father, a union of life with He Who is life.

Ge 2: 16 And the LORD God commanded the man, saying, Of every tree of the garden thou mayest freely eat: 17 But of the tree of the knowledge of good and evil, thou shalt not eat of it: for in the day that thou eatest thereof thou shalt surely die.

What does it mean to be in relationship with God through His covenant? It means to have life itself.

John 11:25 Jesus said unto her, I am the resurrection, and the life: he that believeth in me, though he were dead, yet shall he live:

Do you see this? *He is life.* Not just the temporary act of breathing we experience on this earth, but the real and true life. He is the One who gives all life to mankind. Without being in covenant union with Him, we are dead! It only needs for our heart to stop for us to experience our separation from Him. Those who are not united to Him are in a state of death.

What does it mean when we are baptized into Him? Nothing less than being born-again, that is, the receiving of a new life, which is being in Him. When we are baptized, we are taken out of complete and total involvement in Adam and placed in Christ while still living in this flesh. [51] This creates the war between the two natures which Paul talks about in the epistles. Our organic and fleshly unity with Adam pulls us towards sin, but the righteousness, which lives within us as the new man in Christ, pulls us towards Christ and living for Him. A mere declaration of belief would not have such an effect. Nowhere in the Bible are we given the idea of a covenant with God being made through the saying of a Sinner's Prayer.

I believe it is possible, through the mercy of God given to those who act in good will but in ignorance, to be saved. Our loving Father wishes that all come to Him, and we cannot put a limit on His mercy. But those who find a relationship with Christ through making a decision for Christ are in a truncated relationship which does not have the fullness of salvation, and finds them opposing the very Sacraments which would deepen their walk with Christ.

---

[51] **Rom. 6: 3**

ETERNAL LIFE – This is where the real confusion about our salvation takes place. In talking with both Catholics and Protestants, people speak of salvation as having eternal life, and eternal life as being "saved." For Protestants especially, this leads to the belief that once one is saved, i.e. taken from being in Adam to being in Christ through "making a decision for Jesus," one now has an absolute assurance of eternal life. To this I must say as loudly as possible:

IT MOST CERTAINLY DOES NOT!

At least, *not* in the way those who toss those terms around mean it to be. To Evangelicals, salvation, born again, and redemption are words which all mean we have been given the gift of eternal life which can never be forfeited or given away by us. More than one Evangelical preacher has been heard to say if people have made a "decision for Jesus" they should be *as sure of heaven as if already there.*" This violates the principles of covenant. When we are baptized into Christ, we make oaths (or our parents make these oaths on our behalf if we are baptized as children) and we will be judged by whether or not we have kept these oaths.

Romans 2:7 To them who by patient continuance in well doing seek for glory and honour and immortality, eternal life:

What is the point of patient continuance in well doing if we already have eternal life and nothing can take that away from us? Romans makes it clear that salvation is a life-long process of keeping our covenant vows so as to receive the blessed life. The context of Romans 2 shows that the reception of eternal life is contingent upon the works we do here on earth during our lifetime. There is no idea of a separate judgment seat for believers only where they are rewarded with gifts according to their faithfulness. That is another fatuous Protestant invention.

There is one judgment only. I do not see anywhere in Scripture the idea of two separate and distinct judgments of Christ, one for the wicked and one for the believer.

At the Judgment Seat spoken of in Matthew 25, we see those who have done good (believers) and also of those who have done evil (unbelievers). They are both at the same judgment seat. Now if being "saved" means you receive irrevocable eternal life, then how do we find believers at the Judgment Seat of Christ to receive eternal life for their good deeds?

I can just hear someone now saying *"Heretic! Now you are teaching salvation by works!"*

You weren't paying attention. Go back and read again what I just wrote. Salvation is the state of being saved from the general condemnation of being in Adam. It is accomplished by one Person alone. Christ Jesus our Lord. Only He could make the New Covenant. We had nothing to do with that. No man could aid Him in any way in accomplishing this covenant. Our works do not save us. Period. It would be works to insist we had anything to do with the redeeming of mankind as a whole from the condemnation of Adam and thus saved ourselves from damnation by establishing a new covenant with God.

The problem with the idea of once saved – always saved is that people do not know that salvation is a covenant, or do not understand how a covenant works. I have seen some strange descriptions of covenant on the Internet. We make it with our Lord Jesus Christ, through Whom we enter into the *family* through an oath by which we pledge to be faithful to the end of our lives. The *family covenant* has a blessing promised for those who indeed remain faithful. That blessing is our inheritance in Christ. This is in keeping with the analogy of the family, for just as in an earthly family there is an inheritance for good children, in the family of God there is also an inheritance, eternal life.

Eph 1:11 In whom also we have *obtained an inheritance*, being

76

predestinated according to the purpose of him who worketh all things after the counsel of his own will:

Eph 1:14 Which is the earnest of our inheritance until the redemption of the purchased possession, unto the praise of his glory.

Eph 1:18 The eyes of your understanding being enlightened; that ye may know what is the hope of his calling, and what the riches of the glory of his inheritance in the saints,

Our Lord also spoke of inheriting the kingdom.

Matthew 19:29 And every one that hath forsaken houses, or brethren, or sisters, or father, or mother, or wife, or children, or lands, for my name's sake, shall receive an hundredfold, and shall *inherit* everlasting life.

Do people inherit everlasting life by having faith alone? I don't see it in scripture. Even the most cursory reading of this text shows Christ is not afraid to attach certain conditions, expressed in *works of faith*, to this covenant inheritance, and never mentions nor says the words "faith alone."

Matthew 25:34 Then shall the King say unto them on his right hand, Come, ye blessed of my Father, *inherit the kingdom* prepared for you from the foundation of the world:

In the context of the rest of the verses in this passage, by what standard does the King say unto these that they may receive the inheritance? By the standard of works of love, charity, and grace which they have *done* in their lives.

So much for sola fide and a "decision for Jesus" giving us eternal life. Salvation and entrance into the kingdom, yes. You cannot earn that. That is by grace alone though faith. Eternal life, no. Faith moves us to the act of baptism, which is the entrance into the covenant. But as I am showing you now, faith alone will not confer eternal life to the soul. The verses I am quoting show the necessity of doing works, for it is by our good works that we keep our covenant with Christ and obtain the promised inheritance.

Mark 10:17 And when he was gone forth into the way, there came one running, and kneeled to him, and asked him, Good Master, what shall I do that I may *inherit eternal life*?

Luke 10:25 And, behold, a certain lawyer stood up, and tempted him, saying, Master, what shall I do to *inherit* eternal life?

Luke 18:18 . . . Good Master, what shall *I do to inherit* eternal life?

Go to these verses. Study Christ's response. Jesus always rebuked erroneous understandings of God and the OT scriptures, yet in none of His responses do we see a rebuke of this idea of doing something to inherit eternal life. Here is a bully chance for Christ to rebuke this understanding if it is erroneous and *He does not.* He responds to the question with an answer in which He states what must be *done* to inherit eternal life.

Here are two more verses showing the inheritance of eternal life is received on the Judgment Day when we are proven to have been covenant keepers rather than covenant breakers.

1Corinthians 6:9 Know ye not that the unrighteous shall not *inherit* the kingdom of God? Be not deceived: neither fornicators, nor idolaters,

78

nor adulterers, nor effeminate, nor abusers of themselves with mankind,

1Corinthians 6:10 Nor thieves, nor covetous, nor drunkards, nor revilers, nor extortioners, shall *inherit* the kingdom of God.

Notice who does not inherit the kingdom. It is those who **do evil**. What do covenant breakers inherit? In Deuteronomy 28:1-14, God promises blessing to covenant keepers. In verses 15-68, covenant-breakers are promised curse. This is principle number four of Sutton's covenant paradigm, oaths and sanctions.

This picture of earthly covenant blessing and curse is a picture of what happens in the next life. Covenant keepers are blessed. Covenant breakers are cursed. There is no idea, either in the Old Covenant or the New Covenant of simply becoming a believer and then everything is settled once and for all. That is a fond invention which comes from the Western idea of salvation as a legal transaction.

Roman Catholicism is directly to blame for this. The soteriological ideas of the Western Church were directly influenced by the culture of the Roman Empire. This empire was consumed with the understanding of LAW. The law, its practice, understanding, and proper punishment, was everything to the Roman citizen. The law gave the Roman citizen advantages which pagan societies did not have. When St. Paul was being falsely accused and persecuted for the faith, he appealed to Roman law and demanded his rights under that law as a citizen of Rome.

From this law-based idea of salvation, which stands in contradiction to the Eastern view of salvation as medicine and not legal declaration, Protestantism developed the idea of forensic (legal) justification. A sinner repents, says a prayer of repentance, and in heaven, his sins are blotted out and he is declared once and forever legally not guilty before God. Taken to a logical conclusion, the saved sinner can then not worry about his life because he is home free in regard to heaven.

Orthodoxy does not treat salvation like this. Salvation for us is a return to God's original plan for us – that we would become gods. [52] This means that salvation involves more than just a heavenly declaration of legal innocence. It is a complete change of our very being so that over the course of our earthly life, we become like Christ. All that we do in Orthodoxy as part of our journey into theosis – the fasting, the prayers, the Sacraments – are designed to aid us in this change. A person who follows the teaching of the Church is keeping his covenant with God through the Church. At the Judgment Seat of Christ, he will be blessed as a covenant keeper. Those who do not wish to be troubled with such matters will find on that day that they are internally unchanged, and will have to go through the fire of God's purging, a most painful process. [53]

A parallel verse to this is found in the book of Romans. Romans 2: 7 clearly states those who **do good** are the recipients of eternal life and immortality.

1Co 15:50 Now this I say, brethren, that flesh and blood *cannot inherit* the kingdom of God; neither doth corruption inherit incorruption. Ga 5:21 Envyings, murders, drunkenness, revellings, and such like: of the which I tell you before, as I have also told you in time past, that they which do such things shall *not inherit* the kingdom of God.

Heb 6:12 That ye be not slothful, but followers of them who through

---

[52] "God became man that man might become God." St. Athanasius in his work On The Incarnation.

[53]

1Corinthians 3:13 Every man's work shall be made manifest: for the day shall declare it, because it shall be revealed by fire; and the fire shall try every man's work of what sort it is. 14 If any man's work abide which he hath built thereupon, he shall receive a reward. 15 If any man's work shall be burned, he shall suffer loss: but he himself shall be saved; yet so as by fire.

faith and patience _inherit_ the promises.

Faith is the foundation upon which our works of covenant obedience are done. It is the energizing force which propels us to those works. It is that which God sees as righteousness. James says faith has works. Works are, in fact, the icon of our unseen faith, just as the icons in our church show us the presence of the unseen saints who commune with the church.

1 Pe 3:9 Not rendering evil for evil, or railing for railing: but contrariwise blessing; knowing that ye are there unto called, that ye should _inherit_ a blessing.

Re 21:7 He that overcometh shall _inherit_ all things; and I will be his God, and he shall be my son.

Even Evangelicals and Fundamentalists question the status of believers who are disobedient and live in sin and rebellion against God. They understand obedience is a sign of one's being in the kingdom. What they do not understand is that in a covenant format, as shown by the verses above, obedience is the way in which we keep the covenant oaths we made in baptism. Thus, as good and faithful covenant keeping children, we inherit the fullness of the redemptive work Christ did on behalf of mankind, eternal life. Disobedience does not mean one has never been born again. It means one is a covenant breaker and unless there is true repentance, he stands to be _disinherited_ on the Last Day.

Remember my opening statement about God using analogy of things common to mankind to teach us of heavenly realities? The family inheritance is one of those realities. On earth, honorable children receive inheritance and dishonorable ones are disinherited. The child who is rebellious, wicked, and brings shame upon the family name is _disinherited._ He receives no blessing from the family inheritance. This is exactly how the inheritance of Christ's covenant works with us. The blessing of the covenant is eternal life. The curse is to be sent out of the household of God and into painful chastisement.

REDEMPTION: Christ redeems mankind by the establishment of a New Covenant to replace the Old Covenant. He pays the price of redemption for Adam's sin. Thus a new mankind is created, one which is in covenant with the Father. Redemption is corporate for mankind.

SALVATION: The state of individually being saved from the condemnation of our organic (fleshly) union with our father Adam. We are flesh of his flesh, bone of his bone, and therefore, in this intimate union, share in the condemnation of his flesh. When we are baptized, making covenant with Christ, we are taken out of the old Adam and placed in the Last Adam. Thus are we indeed saved from condemnation. We leave Adam and enter Christ.

BORN AGAIN: The receiving of new life. That life is Christ. Being placed in Christ by baptism [54] we are taken out of a life which is one of death (Adam) and placed into a life which is one of Life (Christ). Since the typology of being born, in human experience, is that of receiving life, this understanding is proper to what is really happening. We are being made alive by birth through the waters of baptism. As newborn children we are adopted into the Father's kingdom family and have the inheritance waiting for us.

ETERNAL LIFE: Eternal life is the *inheritance* of the covenant family. It has been obtained for us by our Elder Brother, Christ Jesus. Not only does He procure it, but according to John 17:2 and other verses, it is He Who

---

[54] **Rom 6: 3-4 and Gal. 3: 27**

82

will be in charge of dispensing the inheritance on the Great Judgement Day to those He judges to be faithful covenant keepers. This follows perfectly the covenant pattern found in the patriarchal families of the Old Covenant. The eldest son was the one who administered the covenant and its blessings upon the death of the covenant head of the family, the father of the clan.

I must address one more word which is more common to Calvinists than any other Protestant. Calvinists are fond of describing individuals as being either *regenerate* or *unregenerate* when talking of a person's spiritual state. Yet this word <u>doesn't even exist</u> in scripture, which puts our sola scriptura friends in a strange position indeed. There is neither Scriptural warrant to talk of individuals in this manner, nor any history of the Church in which salvation is understood in this manner. The only close word found in the Bible is *regeneration,* and is understood corporately. It refers to the work of Christ in which the Creation is redeemed to God and the kosmos is restored to Him. The Greek for this word is παλιγγενεσα (*palinogenesis*), and it means literally to "re-genesis" Do you see the connection here between Jesus as the Last Adam and His re-genesis of Creation in the work of redemption?

Therefore, regeneration is ongoing, the work of Christ which continues through the work of His Body on earth, the Church, and which will come to completion upon His return at the end of time. Regeneration is not applied to individuals in the way Calvinists present it. It is a horrible piece of eisegesis.

SUMMARY

I have tried to show the way in which Evangelicals and Fundamentalists confuse the redemptive work of our Lord by intermingling the definitions for His work, making different words have the same meaning. Their definitions break the covenant principles by which God deals with us as his children. The redemption plan is already in place. We enter into it by making covenant with Christ through the means which He has chosen – baptism into the kingdom family. Thus we become adopted children in the family covenant. If we remain faithful children, growing in grace and righteousness, we can expect to receive the great and unspeakable inheritance of light which our Savior alone has procured for us. Remember that eternal life is a family inheritance, not a legal decree of absolute forgiveness no matter what we do while here on earth.

THE COVENANT FAMILY
AT WORSHIP

On any given Sunday anywhere in the world, it is possible to go to an immense variety of churches and ecclesial assemblies and participate in a staggering variety of forms of worship. Was this the intention of our Father, or did He have a particular form of worship in mind? Which of the thousands of worship forms most resembles that which was originally given to mankind and what is the significance of that worship? I think these are important questions.

I wish to begin by tossing out certain forms of worship at the beginning of this discourse. Anything with drums, guitars, tambourines, and loud, thumping music is not the worship the Lord ordained. The experience being had in these ecclesial assemblies is one of being entertained. If it sounds like it belongs in a nightclub . . . it probably does. In many of these so called "mega-churches," exciting the flesh is often described as a movement of the Holy Spirit. If the Holy Spirit is moving in these services in healing people, it is because God is so good, so full of love, so merciful, that he will meet hearts truly hungry for Him in any circumstance. That circumstance does not necessarily have to be Orthodox Christianity. This may well be the love of God expressed to sinful human beings for His own purpose, but it is not the worship He ordained.

Where then do we find the worship He ordained? We begin in Genesis!

Hebrews 8:5 Who serve unto the example and shadow of heavenly things, as Moses was admonished of God when he was about to make the tabernacle: for, See, saith he, that thou make all things according to the pattern shewed to thee in the mount.

Here we see the beginnings of the family worship which our Father first established in the desert with His Old Covenant people, national Israel. There was a specific place of worship – the wilderness tabernacle. Within that specific place there were specific items of worship ordained by God. The whole edifice was constructed according to plans shown to Moses, and Hebrews 8: 5 says God *admonished* Moses to follow this pattern. The word *"admonished"* carries a much greater force than to just tell someone to do something in a certain way. It is akin to God sticking a finger in Moses' nose and giving him a dire warning. Why was God so concerned that man not make additions to the pattern shown Moses in the mountain?

Hebrews 9:23 It was therefore necessary that the *patterns of things in the heavens* should be purified with these; but the heavenly things themselves with better sacrifices than these. 24 For Christ is not entered into the holy places made with hands, *which are the figures of the true*; but into heaven itself, now to appear in the presence of God for us:

It is because the tabernacle and the worship conducted therein would be a visible representation of the true worship in heaven. The earthly tabernacle and the worship which goes on inside it are figures (types) of the eternal true worship which takes place in heaven. Every Jewish liturgical service which took place was a testimony – both to Jews and the unbelieving pagans who witnessed it – of the heavenly truths of the spiritual realm.

The word "liturgy" means "the work of the people." It does not mean to in any way provide entertainment. Solid and orthodox worship is *work* – it demands from us our full participation and attention and which involves a certain degree of discomfort. In the Liturgy of St. John Chrysostom, the first prayer of the Liturgy of the Eucharist [55] says: *"Let us, who mystically represent the cherubim and sing the thrice-holy hymn to the life-giving trinity, **lay aside all worldly cares**, that we may receive the King of all, invisibly escorted by the angelic hosts. Alleluia, alleluia, alleluia."* [56]

In other words, it is time to stop daydreaming and start paying close attention, something very important is about to happen. How important is the Liturgy of the Eucharist, which begins with the chanting of the Cherubic Hymn?

Here is an incredible story about Euthymios the Great which took place after the start of the Cherubic Hymn.

"All the monks were present, all of them without exceptions, suddenly saw a huge flame coming from above, from the temple's dome, like a sheet that was covering, like a flaming cloud, surrounding Euthymios the Great along with Father Dometianos in the Holy Bema.

A fearful sight . . . and even more fearful, when they saw them realizing the Great entrance was surrounded by flames, moving within them and with

---

[55] All Catholic liturgies are divided into two parts: the Liturgy of the Word, which ends with the reading of the Gospel and the homily, and the Liturgy of the Eucharist which follows the homily.

[56] This prayer is known as the Cherubikon or the Cherubic Prayer.

them . . .

Everyone fell on their stomach, for they could not bear the light and the brightness coming from the flames, in which those two worthy Celebrants were wrapped . . .

This reminds us of the Lord's Transfiguration on Mount Tabor. I should shout: "Oh, how miserable are today's young priests!"

The two celebrants, flame bearing and light bearing, remained in this state until the end of the Divine Liturgy.

Indeed it was awesome, when it was time for the monks to receive Holy Communion, how did they go for communion while witnessing this fearful sight? With trembling feet, with dazzled eyes, with awe from within, amazement and in peace and rejoicing in their hearts . . . The heaven, paradise, the Triumphant Church, the Jerusalem Above, the Glory of our Christ, all were present, all within them . . . And all inside us . . . for that is how it happens, even if we do not see it. Inconceivable beauty and inexpressible blessedness, which was experienced by those who were partakers of that Divine Liturgy! How can one describe that which "eye has not seen, nor ear heard"? But in fact they saw, heard and experienced, that which was allowed by God to those chosen living earthen vessels. " [57]

Didn't a similar thing happen when Moses finished and consecrated the tabernacle in the wilderness?

Exd 40:33 And he reared up the court round about the tabernacle and the altar, and set up the hanging of the court gate. So Moses finished the work. 34 Then a cloud covered the tent of the congregation, and the glory

---

[57] The Great Synaxarion of the Orthodox Church I Vol 1 - Athens 1992 I Pg. 495 from Experiences in the Divine Liturgy I Pg. 221-222

of the LORD filled the tabernacle. 35 And Moses was not able to enter into the tent of the congregation, because the cloud abode thereon, and the glory of the LORD filled the tabernacle. 36 And when the cloud was taken up from over the tabernacle, the children of Israel went onward in all their journeys: 37 But if the cloud were not taken up, then they journeyed not till the day that it was taken up. 38 For the cloud of the LORD was upon the tabernacle by day, and fire was on it by night, in the sight of all the house of Israel, throughout all their journeys.

Worship is not just something we do once a week, a place where we can forget about our cares and worries because the service and the music make us feel good. My happiness is not the primary duty of the Liturgy, although one may certainly leave Liturgy with the profound refreshment of soul which comes from having experienced the love of God for us poor sinners. No, Liturgy is the joining of this mundane and sad earth to the glorious worship ever eternal in heaven. The monks at worship with Euthymios the Great experienced an event which the majority of us will never in our lifetimes either see or experience. They entered into the heavenly reality which takes place during the Liturgy.

Does it fill you with a sense of majesty and awe to read of the appearance of the Lord in the tabernacle in the wilderness and similarly at the Divine Liturgy celebrated by Euthymios the Great? I fear that for the great majority of us, modern man has lost the sense of the very real presence of God in our worship. We do not see, therefore, we do not believe with all our hearts. And if we do not believe with all our hearts, then the next step is to turn the worship into something we can believe in.

This was exactly what God did not wish to happen to the service of the tabernacle. No wonder God sternly warned Moses not to be twiddling with the worship to make it more palatable to human desire. Worship here on earth never has been and never should be about being entertained.

Seeing that we are participating and sharing in the worship of heaven, let us look at the heavenly worship to see which of the thousands of worship experiences looks most like that which is seen in heaven.

What God established in Jewish worship is a pattern of that which is in heaven, therefore, the idea that God would ask us to totally leave the heavenly pattern He established in Judaism is unthinkable. Here is a sample of a writer who only sees the sarcedotal system as being manmade and false. While it was said about Roman Catholic worship, it applies equally to Orthodoxy

"The entire system of Catholic worship is built by copying the Old Testament rabbinical system. It incorporates a priesthood and sacrifices that negate the work of Christ done on the Cross. There are masses, indulgences, last rites, stations of the cross, the Rosary, and numerous other works to pay for the sins of the faithful. Such practices are rooted in the shadow system of the Old Testament that looked forward to Christ. Catholics observe the shadow and ignore the substance."

This writer does not understand that in the New Covenant, Christ brings substance to the shadow so that now the shadow becomes reality. Because worship in the New Covenant congregation is a continuation of that which God began with Moses in the wilderness, that is exactly why it *should* look like Judaism! It is not copying the Old Testament rabbinical system, but rather having it continue in the fullness of Christ.

With this in mind, let's look at some individual parts of Orthodox worship with which Protestants have serious reservations.

PRIESTS

As part of the authority structure of the covenant family, God established

90

a priesthood to serve His people in His congregation. What is a priest?

Several definitions I have read point to the same idea: a priest is a representative, one who represents both ways – God to people and people to God. He intercedes on behalf of sinners by the administration of the Sacraments, and He speaks the truth of God to sinners to guide and direct them into wise choices in following God's will for their lives.

The first priest was Adam. Why do I say this? Because he represented not only mankind, but all of Creation before God. It was not only as covenant head, but also as priest he failed. He did not represent God to Eve, both as her protector in resisting the evil one, and the one who spoke boldly God's word. Thus, as a representative of God, he failed.

I believe Noah acted as a priest to the world around him. Every board he put into place, every animal he round up for the ark, spoke for God and represented God's coming action to a doomed world: God is going to judge you for your sins. Repent and enter into the ark for salvation. Even without the ordinances and temple ceremonies which would come later as God established them in the desert with Moses, Noah still acted as representative.

When the ark finally landed and the earth dried up, what did Noah do? He acted as priest by offering the prescribed sacrifices. These blood sacrifices cleansed and renewed the covenant. Noah acted as priest, a covenant representative between creation and God. This is also how we, as believers, act as priests to a dying world around us. Our lives and actions, when inspired by and following the truth of the scriptures, speak God's truth and warning to the world around us.

When God established His kingdom on earth, national Israel He said *"And ye shall be unto me a kingdom of priests, and an holy nation. These are the words which thou shalt speak unto the children of Israel."* [58]

---

[58] **Exodus 19:6**

Almost the identical same words are found in 1 Peter 2: 9 regarding the New Covenant Israel: *"But ye are a chosen generation, a royal priesthood, an holy nation, a peculiar people; that ye should shew forth the praises of him who hath called you out of darkness into his marvelous light."* God's people, His family on earth, are all priests because we represent Him and His truth.

Unfortunately, this truth is misrepresented by those who do not accept the sacerdotal and mediatorial priesthood. The claim is made that by the fact that all believers are priests, there is no more need for a special class of ordained priests with God given powers to administer the Sacraments. Is this so?

Scripture seems to teach otherwise. The pattern of the heavenly started in the Old Testament continues in the New. There is no indication in the scriptures of the mediatorial priesthood of the Levites being discontinued with the coming of Christ. God gives to the Levitical priests in the OT the representational authority to present offerings which forgive sin and renewed an individual's covenant with God. [59] Christ our God gives to His Apostles in the NT the same authority in greater measure, for not only can they offer the appropriate offering for sin – the Eucharist – they can also hear sin confessed and pronounce God's forgiveness upon the offender, thus restoring covenant relationship between the sinner and God. [60]

This is a pattern which is found throughout the NT. The ceremonies and offices of the OT are brought forward to the NT and changed as they are fulfilled in Christ. For instance, Passover becomes Eucharist. Circumcision becomes Baptism. In each case, the OT shadow is fulfilled in Christ and the new ritual not only accomplishes that which the old only signified, it gives greater blessings.

---

[59] Exodus 29:36; Leviticus 4:14; Numbers 15:24 & others

[60] John 20:23

Gen.14: 18 *"And Melchizedek king of Salem brought forth bread and wine: and he was the priest of the most high God."*

Beginning with Melchizedek in Genesis 14, we see a distinct class of men who are called to a priesthood which is outside the normal realm of the priesthood of all believers. The actions of Melchizedek point to, as do many OT types, a future fulfilment in Christ and His Church. Look at what Melchizedek does: he brings forth bread and wine! Who else do we know brings forth bread and wine to the people? The priests of the Orthodox Church. To what purpose did Melchizedek perform this offering? I think a clue is found in the next chapter.

Abram speaks to God, expressing his concern that he has no heir to the promised blessings. God's response is to establish His covenant with Abram:

Genesis 15:5 *And he brought him forth abroad, and said, Look now toward heaven, and tell the stars, if thou be able to number them: and he said unto him, So shall thy seed be.*

This is Sutton's first principle of covenant making – transcendence. The greater offers covenant to the lesser. During this offering there is the recitation of all the great deeds God. This is known as the covenant preamble, which identifies the Lordship of the Great King and stresses His greatness, dominance and eminence. God brings Abram out and shows him the majesty of who He is by the witness of His creative work.

Genesis 15: 7 *And he said unto him, I am the LORD that brought thee out of Ur of the Chaldees, to give thee this land to inherit it.*

This is a part of the first principle of covenant called the historical prologue. It is a recounting of the Great King's previous relationship to the lesser one, with special emphasis on the benefits or blessing of that relationship. God reminds Abram that by His power and protection, Abram has been led out of the pagan land of his birth and into a place of blessing and plenty, and a relationship in which there are incredible promises of blessings yet to come.

Genesis 15:8 *And he said, Lord God, whereby shall I know that I shall inherit it?*

Abram now looks for the guarantee, made by an oath, which takes place in any covenant cutting ritual.

Genesis 15: 9 *And he said unto him, Take me an heifer of three years old, and a she goat of three years old, and a ram of three years old, and a turtledove, and a young pigeon. 10 And he took unto him all these, and divided them in the midst, and laid each piece one against another: but the birds divided he not.*

Genesis 15: 17 *And it came to pass, that, when the sun went down, and it was dark, behold a smoking furnace, and a burning lamp that passed between those pieces.*

This is the heart of cutting a covenant. God promises seed as numerous as the stars and land. God then puts Abram in a deep sleep and passes through the pieces of the slaughtered animals. Why do this? Because in a covenant, when oaths are made, self-maledictory sanctions are part of the oath making process. God is saying by the action of passing through the carcasses, *"If I fail to do all I have promised to do here, may the same be done to me as to these animals."*

Protestants have taken these verses in Genesis 15 as an indication of

94

their "sola fide" position on salvation, claiming they show God alone Who does everything, and we do nothing to become saved. This idea violates the marital analogy of a covenant in which both sides choose the other as an act of free will, and both parties make their own vows with self-maledictory oaths. If both sides do not enter freely into the covenant relationship, there is no covenant. Therefore, it is impossible that God cut covenant for both sides of the covenant.

They also miss the fact that the response of Abram to perform his part comes two chapters later. In Genesis 17, we find God calling Abram to his part of the covenant relationship. Once again the promises of God's faithfulness to this relationship are recited, and this time, Abram is told what he must do to enter into the covenant relationship with God. God has already established His self-maledictory oath in Genesis 15, passing through the slain animals. Now Abram is renamed and he takes an action which is a self-maledictory oath: he performs the act of circumcision. In circumcision, the Jewish male bore a sign on his body which said *"If I fail to keep all that I have vowed to the Lord, may I be cut off from Him as this flesh was cut off."*

From Melchizedek onward, we see God orders, as part of the worship which is pleasing to Him, the ordination of a class of men who are to serve the function of priest in a special way. These men are to offer the ordinances of the Lord in national Israel. They will lead the people in worship, confession of sin, and all the other ceremonies which particularly belong to national Israel as God's people. I speak, of course, of the Levitical priesthood, which began with Aaron and his sons being consecrated for the service of the Lord. Following Aaron came the consecration of the Levites to the service of the Lord:

Num 8:10 And thou shalt bring the Levites before the LORD: and the children of Israel shall put their hands upon the Levites: 11 And Aaron shall offer the Levites before the LORD for an offering of the children of Israel, that they may execute the service of the LORD. 12 And the Levites

shall lay their hands upon the heads of the bullocks: and thou shalt offer the one for a sin offering, and the other for a burnt offering, unto the LORD, to make an atonement for the Levites. 13 And thou shalt set the Levites before Aaron, and before his sons, and offer them for an offering unto the LORD. 14 Thus shalt thou separate the Levites from among the children of Israel: and the Levites shall be mine.

Notice how the whole family of God, the children of Israel, are involved in the consecration of the Levites to the priesthood. I want to continually stress the familial nature of our covenant relationship. What a beautiful and yet solemn moment this must have been. Notice what these men are to do; they are to minister to the Lord in a special way the rest of the congregation of Israel cannot. This is the nature of the ordained priesthood. There are services of the Lord which are reserved to certain men only. They are called out from the rest of God's people for the special service of offering sacrifice. There is also a particular office which only one man may hold and in which he offers a sacrifice which no one else may offer. It is the office of high priest.

It is impossible to have proper liturgical and sacramental worship without a priest. There is no evidence from scripture, no verse which specifically says the mediatorial priesthood, with its special authority and responsibility, has ever been abrogated by the work of Christ. In the next chapter I want to go to Sacraments of the Church, which are the special work of the priest in the Liturgy.

The priest as representative agrees with basic Calvinist understanding:

"Representation is inescapable. Van Til observes, "The covenant idea is nothing but the expression of the representative principle consistently applied to all reality." All of creation images God, especially man. And because of sin, man needs a representative to atone for him. Paul explains the representative principle when he says, "For if by the transgression of the one [Adam] the many

96

died, much more did the grace of God and the gift by the grace of one Man, Jesus Christ, abound to many" (Rom. 5:15). Since mankind has no essential unity with God in His being, the human race always needs a representative before God. Christ is that representative." [61]

And therein lies the problem. Calvinist theology makes distinct errors at this very junction. First of all, Christ is not visible to the created world. Yet Sutton says this:

*"Christ is raised and seated in heaven, and then His authority is planted on earth. The Lord declares Christ's transcendence, and then establishes Christ's **visible sovereignty** through the rule of His people as His authority."* [62]

Does Bishop Sutton actually read what he writes? When I read this passage in his book it almost screamed the priesthood at me! It is a open call for the visible authority of the bishops, and the priests in order that God may be represented visibly to this world.

Or does Sutton somehow think that the Church was intended to be a democracy rather than a kingdom? When he speaks of visible authority, is his thinking along the lines of American democracy in which the authority of the land is the vote of the largest mob of people? We are seeing even now the chaos that has entered into the Christian world as each person feels that they, like Martin Luther, have an individual right to act as an all-sufficient authority in matters of theology.

If Christ is absent, He must have a representative in this world who is

---

[61] **THAT YOU MAY PROSPER | Institute for Christian Economics | June 1987 | Pages 46-47.**

[62] **Ibid | Page 45**

visible and speaks with authority on His behalf. That representative is the Church and the authorities who make up the hierarchy of the Church. Only the Church is called the pillar and ground of truth. Every time a Calvinist repeats the Nicene Creed he agrees to doctrines established by the Church a thousand years before Calvin was born, for it was the Church universal (katholicos) which established them.

It is the Church, with the visible authority of the bishops who are successors of the Apostles and their authority, who give authority to the priests. Priests in turn, do not speak on their own behalf, but are to speak that which the Church has determined as truth through the authority of the bishops and the ecumenical councils in which they met over the centuries to oppose heresy and hammer out truth for the people of God.

By saying that Christ alone is that representative, Calvinists try to deconstruct the necessity for the sacerdotal priesthood, claiming that there is no more need for the priesthood, since Christ represents us to God with a perfect sacrifice. Here is their problem:

Protestants accuse us of denying the sufficiency of Christ's sacrifice by offering Him in sacrifice in the Liturgy. They point to verses such as Hebrews 10:10, which talk about a sacrifice that is done once and sanctifies us forever. But they utterly miss the context of this verse, for in the previous three chapters leading up to Hebrews 10:10, Christ is being discussed not as a Levitical priest, but as our Great High Priest. They are confusing the covenant sacrifice of Yom Kippor, which was done only on behalf of the covenant congregation to renew that corporate covenant, with the peace offerings and the daily sacrifice for sin which was given for individual sins.

The high priest alone could offer Yom Kippor, and Yom Kippur was not for personal sins. The Levitical priesthood offered peace offerings unto God for the individual sins of individual people. I hope you see the difference. Yom Kippor is the corporate covenant offering. Hebrews 10:10 is talking about the sacrifice of Yom Kippor, offered once and applied once and forever instead of yearly. That is the entire context of chapters seven to ten of Hebrews – the Great High Priesthood of Christ. I find nowhere in the NT which redefines the nature of the OT peace offering to be now once and done for the individual sinner. We must, therefore, assume that just as the peace offering for sin was offered whenever the sinner knew he had sinned and needed to be covenantally restored to God, the NT peace offering, the Holy Eucharist, be offered to God on a continuing basis to deal with our daily covenant violations and restore us to God.

The idea of a once and for all sacrifice as described by Evangelicals really means *once applied.* This is the logical result of the legal fiction called "imputed righteousness." After all, if you are declared righteous by a divine legal fiat, then you don't really need any further sacrifice, do you? In Protestant thinking, the "once and done forever" sacrifice of Christ takes care of everything for the believer. One just has to believe. Unfortunately for them, the verses in Romans which are appealed to by those believing in imputed righteousness are mistranslated. When we sin and break our covenant with Christ, we need a sacrifice to restore the covenant relationship.

This is why we refer to the Eucharist in sacrificial terms. Remember, covenants are established with sacrifice. They are also *restored* with sacrifice and enlarged upon with sacrifice. Whenever God took the covenant promises given to Abraham and enlarged upon them, you will find sacrifice involved. Blood is always shed in cutting covenant with God, which is why we are not mandated to circumcise our children anymore. The Blood of the New Covenant has been shed, the covenant with mankind is ratified between God and mankind and is permanent. But we must renew our individual and personal covenant with Christ when we break it, and restore it from the damage done to it by sin. If we do not repent of our covenant breaking (sins), and do not offer the appropriate Sacrifice, we stand the chance of being declared unfaithful children on the Judgement Day and sent from the family and its communion.

The only person who can offer such a sacrifice of covenant restoration is a priest, for he alone bears representative authority for Christ, so much so that because Christ indwells him through his ordination, he is known as "alter christus," another Christ. Everywhere you see covenant restoration, you see a representative of that covenant relationship. Christ as Great High Priest has established once and for all an unbreakable covenant between God and His people corporately. This is the "once and for all done" sacrifice. Ours is ongoing. Every time we sin, we need to offer a sacrifice of covenant renewal.

What we do in the Eucharist is in no sense a re-sacrifice of He Who has been once and for all offered. We are simply *applying* that Sacrifice, the same one which John saw in heaven, to our sins. Which is the very same thing which was done under the Old Covenant. Christ's work on the Cross is applied in two ways: a one-time covenant offering for that nation which is the Church, and a continuing Sacrifice which both replaces and is superior to the individual offerings of Israel for the restoration of our covenant and forgiveness of our temporal sins.

Sutton says God must have a visible representative authority. He should pay attention to his own words! An invisible Church is no visible authority!

Sunday Worship

Re 1:10 I was in the Spirit on the Lord's day, and heard behind me a great voice, as of a trumpet,

I want to step out of the mode of disagreeing with Calvinists and address those who claim that Saturday is the only proper day of worship. Besides this verse, there are other references to the meeting of the saints on the first day. The Sabbatarian assemblies are simply wrong to protest that Saturday is the proper day for worship. The Church, acting in the representative authority given Her in

100

our Lord's personal absence, decreed rightly that with the change of covenants came a change of the worship day from Saturday to Sunday. Want to worship on Saturday? Fine. Be ready to accept the condemnation of living in the Old Covenant and keeping the works of the Law, which Christ fulfilled and Paul condemned as being no longer necessary or salvific.

The Sabbath belongs to the Old Covenant. When Christ died, that covenant was done away with. The Sabbath exists no longer. The Sabbath was a particular sign of a particular covenant given to a particular people:

Exd 31:16 Wherefore the children of Israel shall keep the sabbath, to observe the sabbath throughout their generations, [for] a perpetual covenant.

Notice to whom this perpetual covenant was given. The nation of Israel under the Old Covenant. That covenant is finished. Therefore, so is the Sabbath as command for covenant keeping. Like the Passover becoming the Eucharist, the Sabbath rest was changed to Sunday, to celebrate the Lord's Resurrection on the day on which He arose from the dead. My friends who feel that the Sabbath is the day to keep, are you denying the Resurrection without realizing it? [63]

An Altar and Incense

Re 8:3 And another angel came and stood at the altar, having a golden censer; and there was given unto him much incense, that he should

---

[63]
It is important to note that the Hebrew word translated "perpetual" in the KJV is "olam." Olam does not mean either eternal or perpetual, as most of the Western translations indicate. The word "olam" carries the meaning of being off into the distance for an unknown length of time. There are Evangelicals who use this horrible mistranslation to insist that the Jews are still in covenant with God and still His people.

offer it with the prayers of all saints upon the golden altar which was before the throne. 4 And the smoke of the incense, which came with the prayers of the saints, ascended up before God out of the angel's hand.

Remember, God established the worship of His people to be a pattern of the true in heaven. We follow that which has been seen in the reality of John's divine vision. I would simply ask Calvinists and Protestants this: where's your altar and incense? Heaven has an altar and incense, why don't you? Orthodoxy has both because heaven does. In fact, if you come to my Orthodox parish, you will never see a Liturgy which is done without incense. This is one of many practices which makes case for the Orthodoxy being the Bible faith.

Vestments

Re 4:4 And round about the throne were four and twenty seats: and upon the seats I saw four and twenty elders sitting, clothed in white raiment; and they had on their heads crowns of gold.

Re 5:6 And the seven angels came out of the temple, having the seven plagues, clothed in pure and white linen, and having their breasts girded with golden girdles.

What more can I add to this? Look at all the beauty shown in the worship found in heaven, then tell me how anything less, even a nice men's suit, is some how proper clerical attire?

The clerical attire of the Church not only marks the seasons by what one is wearing, for instance, blood red or dark vestments on a feast day of a martyr, but they also designate authority. This follows the pattern of the OT in which the priests had certain garments to wear, but the high priest had a more special garment on which he bore the twelve tribes of Israel on a breastplate over his heart.

The vestments of a deacon separate him and his authority from the laity. Likewise, the vestments of each level of priest and bishop speak of a higher level of authority in the Church. This is consistent with Sutton's principle of representational and visible authority. Without such vestments, there is no visible understanding of those who represent God in a special way.

The Prominence of the Virgin Mary

Revelation 12:1 And there appeared a great wonder in heaven; a woman clothed with the sun, and the moon under her feet, and upon her head a crown of twelve stars:

Crowns indicate authority and royalty. We can only come to the conclusion that the Blessed Virgin is indeed the Queen of Heaven as we see her royal dress, her position of authority as spoken of by being clothed with the sun and having the moon under her feet, and her having a crown, indicating her regal position. We are not wrong to honor her who was honored by God to bear the Most Blessed Son of God. To the charge that we worship her in the same manner in which God is worshiped, I must reply that those making that charge do not understand the difference between veneration and worship. They also do not understand the unity of the saints and the ability we have to ask for the intercession of the saints for our needs. Most of all, they do not see that there is a hierarchy in heaven, in which the Blessed Virgin is the Queen of Angels.

In this light, I find it interesting to remember a Fundamentalist preacher who used to pronounce, with glee bordering on unabashed joy, *"Brothers and*

Sisters, we are going to rule over the angels!" He had no problem ascribing to himself a position of power and glory in heaven. Yet this same man would have a problem with Mary having the same power and glory, She who was the first to experience the blessings of Her Son's death and glorious Resurrection!

Intercession of Angels and Saints

Revelation 8:3 And another angel came and stood at the altar, having a golden censer; and there was given unto him much incense, that he should offer it with the prayers of all saints upon the golden altar which was before the throne. 4 And the smoke of the incense, which came with the prayers of the saints, ascended up before God out of the angel's hand.

Here we see in heaven the prayers of the saints offered on behalf of the Body of Christ. The Body of Christ is not separated by death. There is one Body, not two. Not a Body in heaven and a Body on earth. All believers are united to one another when we are baptized into Christ. In Revelation shows us the picture of both the angels and the saints offering to God the prayers of the saints on earth.

One of the frequent and quite indignant objections to the intercession of the saints is *"The Bible forbids praying to the dead! That's necromancy and it is evil."*

Once again, the answer to this can be found in the covenant and the changes that the New Covenant made to the relationship between God and man. In the Garden, mankind spoke freely with God. There was no separation. Only after the Fall was mankind separated from God, not only by death, but potentially for all eternity. Souls, with a nature corrupted by sin, would have been unable to enter the presence of God. There would have been as much chance of loving union with our Father as a favorable union between fire and water.

Because of this lamentable state of the soul, even the righteous of the Old Covenant could not enter heaven upon death. Covenantally, until Christ went into the heavenly tabernacle and performed Yom Kippur as our Great High Priest, there was no way that any man or woman could be in the presence of God. They were held fast in that separation from God called death, yet being righteous, as Abraham and the many other righteous of the Old Covenant, it would have been unjust for them to enter a place of torment. Therefore, God put them in a place of delight called Paradise until Christ finished His redemption of mankind.

During the Old Covenant age there was no way to communicate with these souls because of the separation between them and the living. Any prayers offered to the dead were seized upon by evil spirits who desired to deceive men into following the evil one with false religious ideas and worship. This is why prayers to the dead were banned. It was a door into a spiritual realm inhabited by demons and covenantally under demonic control.

But when the Yom Kippur of Christ was accepted in heaven, the separation of man and God was ended in Christ. The souls of the righteous were emptied from Paradise to be in heaven in the presence of God. There is now one Body of Christ in which exist the redeemed who have gone on to their reward and those of us who are still working out our journey of salvation in fear and trembling. Since there is no longer any separation, and since the saints in heaven now have put on Christ, meaning that they share in the divine nature in a manner far beyond our understanding, they are able to hear our prayers and present them to the throne of God. The restoration of the covenant family structure between God and man, by the work of Christ in establishing a New Covenant, changed everything. The unity of all believers in Christ is one of those great changes.

Liturgical Worship

Revelation 4:8 And the four beasts had each of them six wings about him; and they were full of eyes within: and they rest not day and night, saying, Holy, holy, holy, Lord God Almighty, which was, and is, and is to come.

Revelation 15:3 And they sing the song of Moses the servant of God, and the song of the Lamb, saying, Great and marvelous are thy works, Lord God Almighty; just and true are thy ways, thou King of saints.

Revelation 19:4 And the four and twenty elders and the four beasts fell down and worshiped God that sat on the throne, saying, Amen; Alleluia.

I never appreciated liturgical worship as a Fundamentalist. To me it was something that was done by rote and was basically meaningless. Only when I came to understand that church was not for my entertainment, but for the worship of God, did I begin to appreciate the sharing here on earth of the heavenly chorus which we will never tire of singing through all eternity. Unlike the worship of certain Protestant assemblies, which appears to be more entertainment based for the laity than worship of God, liturgical worship is for God, not for us. Liturgy alone glorifies God, for it copies that heavenly truth which exists in glory. At the same time, we benefit as we participate. We benefit by having to think about what we are saying and by the grace we receive when we involve our heart and soul in the worship. Most of all we benefit by the grace we receive through the reception of the Sacraments which God has ordained to bless us.

I wish I had the space to go into the rich details of all the prayers in our Orthodox Church. There are the Psalms, which are the music of the Church. There are prayers that glorify the power and authority of our Lord, such as these, recited when the priest is putting on his cuffs:

Right: *Thy right hand, O Lord, has been glorified in power. Thy right hand, O Lord, has shattered the enemies. In the greatness of Thy majesty Thou* *hast overthrown Thy adversaries.*

Left: *Thy hands have made and fashioned me. Give me understanding that I may learn Thy commandments.*

The Litany of Peace lifts up all those for whom our Lord commanded to pray: our leaders, the government, the sick and needy, the Church, and all who have special needs. There is a definite structure so that one knows what is coming, and can participate together with the priest. In this way, through our prayers, we exercise our representative priesthood on behalf of others. It is unlike the Brother Jones Traveling Tongues Road Show and Whiskey Emporium where the center of attention is – Brother Jones! Christ is the center of attention, and the prayers offered show this.

Special times of the year, such as Epiphany, Lent, Christmas, and Theophany, remind us of special events in our Lord's life. We are not captive to subjective preaching whims. Liturgy prevents the pastor of a church from abusing his position. Liturgy is based upon that which the Church has approved in Her authority. Protestantism is filled with thousands of assemblies as the result of the splits which have occurred, often when a pastor decides he has found some new truth and decides that the congregation must share his enthusiasm for it. Some Evangelical pastors preach on variations of the same subject over and over and over again. I remember one assembly where we heard nothing but week after week of right-wing political nonsense cloaked in the name of Jesus. After a while, my wife and I sought another place where we felt we could be fed from the Bible instead of the political ideas of a certain man.

Liturgy keeps men from being the center of attention and instead focuses on Christ and His actions through his saints. Liturgy is especially noteworthy when we celebrate a feast day of one of the Church's martyrs. Such lives lived for Christ challenge us to examine ourselves and to press on to the high calling we have in Christ Jesus, regardless of the cost.

Liturgy does not allow for the Lone Ranger mentality to take over the pulpit. There are set church calendar days and set texts from the scriptures upon which the pastor may preach. The Liturgy in the Orthodox Church points to the Eucharist, whereas the center of attention, and sometimes adulation, in Protestantism, is the wisdom and preaching style of the pastor. Often, the sacrifice which our Lord has provided is secondary to the pastor's ability to preach for long periods of time. In Protestant churches, wisdom is considered the center of worship. Knowledge about God is not a bad thing, but should not take the place of encountering God in the Eucharist and prayer.

Fidelity to the Liturgy also prevents the Church from the liberal habit of taking wicked social practices such as homosexuality and trying to place the approval of God upon these practices. This is one reason why the Church is under a great deal of fire by the wicked. Holy Tradition and Liturgy simply allows no room for the introduction of those ideas which are out of line with the will of God. The doctrinal foundation of worship which is done in this century comes from that which existed 2000 years ago. The Orthodox Church is not bowing down to the sexual and feminist idols of the age and allowing them to intrude into the worship of Christ.

In the Liturgy, the Orthodox Church follows the true worship seen in heaven. How different this is from Evangelicalism. I would ask all who practice differently in worship from where in the Bible they get the pattern for their worship. I don't see any form of Protestant worship anywhere!

You know, I think it would be an awfully good witnessing technique to ask people what they think a church service in heaven would look like. Then, after they have described their own particular brand of Protestant worship, complete with drums, guitars, and tambourines, bring them to the worship shown in Revelation and ask them this:

"Why does the worship of God in heaven look so Orthodox?"

SUMMARY

The worship that God wants is representative. It shows the true worship in heaven. It is not for our entertainment, but for the glory of God by showing to this world the glory of heaven. This is why proper worship is so important. When the emissaries of Prince Vladimir saw the Orthodox worship in the great cathedral Hagia Sophia, they came back and said "We did not know if we were in heaven or on earth, so glorious was their worship." This is how it should be. When we enter a properly ordered church, our sense should be one of awe and silence, of prayer and reverence, not of chatting merrily with everyone around us about last week's potluck supper. When we leave, we should have the inner glow of having been in a place where heaven came down to us, the saints joined us in the heavenly worship, and we truly communed with Christ by having Him enter into us in a real and substantive manner.

SIGNS IN THE
COVENANT FAMILY

The Sacraments are the signs of our covenant relationship. All of the Sacraments involve our participation in the eternal covenant. Our relationship with Christ is covenantal, not dispensational. I find it odd that those people who declare themselves to be Bible believers take such pains to ignore the reality of the covenant language found throughout the Bible, with the word covenant appearing over 280 times in both testaments.

Since our relationship is a covenant, and since Christ is called the Bridegroom, I would like to start at the very point at which we enter into the Church on Holy Saturday (if we are converts) and discuss the Sacraments of Baptism and the Eucharist. You will never find in an Orthodox church any separation between these two Sacraments. Even when we baptize our infants, they will receive a drop of the precious Blood of Christ immediately afterward.

As I discuss these Sacraments, I will try to show the relationship they have with the ordinances of the Old Covenant.

BAPTISM AND THE EUCHARIST

In Judaism, before the nuptial bed is entered into there is an important ceremony which takes place with the bride – the mikveh. This is a ceremonial washing for the removal of ritual impurity and is also used to indicate repentance or change of heart.

Sound familiar? Yes, baptism! Baptism is the mikveh of the New Covenant bride, the believer who is about to be united to Christ. Here is some beautiful information on the mikveh, given by an orthodox Jew.

"Judaism calls for the consecration of human sexuality. It is not enough that intimacy be born of commitment and sworn to exclusivity, it must be sacred. As such, the first mandated time for immersion in the mikvah is at the threshold of marriage.

Mikvah before marriage, strictly speaking, is not contingent upon a commitment to regular observance of Family Purity. Even so, it should not be understood as unrelated to this larger framework. It is simply the first time a Jewish woman is commanded to purify herself in this way. And it is an awesome and auspicious way to start a new life together with one's beloved." [64]

Mikvah in Judaism is seen not only as an act of purification, but also as a sign of repentance, turning from one's old life. In the case of the betrothed, the mikvah symbolizes her turning from the single life under the headship of her

---

[64] **The Mikvah | Rivkah Slonim | http: //www.chabad.org/theJewishWoman/ article_cdo/aid/1541/jewish/The-Mikvah.htm**

father, to a new life with her husband. It is a bath of conversion, highly symbolic of the change in life that is taking place.

"In many ways mikvah is the threshold separating the unholy from the holy, but it is even more. Simply put, immersion in a mikvah signals a change in status – more correctly, an elevation in status. Its unparalleled function lies in its power of transformation, its ability to effect metamorphosis." [65]

Baptism is also part of the self-maledictory oath of covenant. The one being baptized, when being lowered into the waters of baptism, testifies to all who observe *"If I fail to keep all that I have promised, may I be immersed in the eternal grave of death symbolized by this water."* This is the same as the self-maledictory oath of the Old Covenant, which was circumcision.

From the NIV Study Bible: *"If I am not loyal in faith and obedience to the Lord, may the sword of the Lord cut off me and my offspring as I have cut off my foreskin."* Thus Abraham was to place himself under the rule of the Lord as his King, consecrating himself, his offspring and all he possessed to the service of the Lord.

We proceed toward baptism by first making the covenantally required baptismal vows, which are similar to the vows made in the covenant of marriage. In every covenant cutting ritual, there must be an act of vow making, with the attendant oaths/sanctions of the covenant being entered into. No ritual – no covenant. It is that simple. Vows are made based on ethics which are agreed upon by both parties entering into the covenant relationship. In making these vows, we are following the third principle of covenant cutting: ethics.

A covenant is made upon certain promises by both sides to each other.

---

[65] **Ibid**

112

As noted earlier, ancient covenantal rites were often made while invoking certain "curses" which would occur if the covenant was ever broken. Also, during the covenant making process, a meal of some sort was often shared together as a way of "blessing" the covenant. Within the suzerain treaty model, once an oath was made, the oath-taker was expected to keep it. If not, there was a system of sanctions that would be implemented based on the oath that was taken—and then broken. Marriage is much the same way: certain oaths are made during the marriage ceremony, which the covenanting couple is "oath-bound" to keep. For Christians today, the taking of Communion (a shared meal) during the marriage ceremony is the blessing on their covenant. However, when one or the other fails to keep the oath made, the covenant (marriage) is broken and only one of two things can occur: reconciliation, or divorce.[66]

During the process of being a catechumen, the seeker is taught about the expectations which constitute fidelity to God in the anticipated relationship. In my particular catechumen's class, each of the Ten Commandments was discussed in detail. It was understood that to violate any of these rules was an attack on the relationship we would be entering into. Just as adultery severs the relationship between a man and a woman, so certain sins, can sever the relationship between our soul and God. If unrepented of, they will result in an inheritance of covenant curse rather than blessing.

On Holy Saturday, before the ritual of baptism, we were first brought into the nave of the Church where we recited certain vows. Here is a copy of a baptismal formula which may be used in the Church on Holy Saturday. These are the promises I made, along with six other catechumens, on April 14th, 2001, when I entered St. Ann Byzantine Catholic Church:

V. Do you renounce Satan? R. I do.

V. And all his works? R. I do.

V. And all his empty show? R. I do.

V. Do you believe in God, the Father Almighty, Creator of heaven and earth? R. I do.

V. Do you believe in Jesus Christ, his only Son, our Lord, who was born of the Virgin Mary, suffered death and was buried, rose again from the dead and is seated at the right hand of the Father? R. I do.

V. Do you believe in the Holy Spirit, the holy Catholic church, the communion of saints, the forgiveness of sins, the resurrection of the body, and life everlasting? R. I do.

V. And may almighty God, the Father of our Lord Jesus Christ, who has given us new birth by water and the Holy Spirit and bestowed on us forgiveness of our sins, keep us by his grace, in Christ Jesus our Lord, for eternal life. R. Amen.

The are the same in the Orthodox Church. By these vows, I was promising fidelity to my Lord through the ministry of His Church and all that She teaches. I also understood, through intense study which included Bishop Sutton's book, that these vows were of a self-maledictory nature. I hope you see the similarity of these vows wedding vows.

Vows, or oaths, are the fourth principle of covenant making. Both parties vow fidelity to the covenant ethics. If the vows are broken, the covenant is broken, and if the violation is severe enough, it may be permanently over, depending upon the willingness of the offended party to forgive. An example of such covenant vow making, with the corresponding promises of blessing for faithfulness and curse for unfaithfulness, can be found in Deuteronomy 28.

Bible Fundamentalists are fond of calling baptism "works salvation." This misnomer shows their complete lack of understanding of the covenant nature of our relationship to the Lord and how a covenant is made. In Fundamentalism, there is an idea that an action called "making a decision for Jesus" has the full weight of bringing salvation, and thus the unbreakable promise of eternal life, to the individual who goes up the aisle of the Baptist church on Sunday morning. This is not possible, for several reasons:

1. Making a "decision for Jesus" involves no ritual of covenant making. There is no instance of anyone ever making a covenant without being personally involved in a ritual in which the principles of the covenant were followed. There must be an act of taking vows and agreeing to the sanctions involved for breaking those vows.

2. Making a "decision for Jesus" can be done in front of one's TV set while watching Billy Graham given an invitation to "invite Jesus into your heart." In such a situation, there is no one watching. But in making a covenant, there must be witnesses to the covenant. Sutton states that the need for witnesses is to bring a covenant lawsuit against anyone who violates the ethics of the covenant. To cut a covenant, three elements are necessary: sanctions, oath, and witnesses. [67] None of these things are present in the act of "making a decision for Jesus."

3. Making a decision for Jesus does not involve the human body. This is an important consideration in covenant cutting. The whole person is given to the other, body, soul, and spirit. The act of involving our body in covenant making, whether it be in circumcision or in baptism, makes real the fact that we as persons are tripartite beings. To withhold my body from the covenant making ritual is to hold back a part of me. Protestants have a strange and almost semi-Gnostic aversion to anything physical being involved in Christian worship, whether it be the body in baptism, or candles, priestly robes, or icons.

---

[67] **THAT YOU MAY PROSPER | Ray Sutton | Institute for Christian Economics | June 1987 | Page 78**

In the baptismal ceremony, catechumens first vow fidelity to the teachings of the Church, and then declare their fidelity to Christ by turning to face West and symbolically spitting at the devil! Thus the betrothal vows to Christ are made. The baptism of converts which follows is the cutting of the covenant in which the marriage declared in front of a church full of witnesses. A spiritually dead sinner goes into the water, is buried with Christ, and is raised a new man in Christ. We now belong to him. The final Sacrament of this momentous day is the receiving of the Eucharist, which is analogous to the nuptial bed, where the covenant is finalized.

When the couple leaves the church, there is traditionally a wedding feast, yet I would bet that most people do not understand the symbolism of such a meal.

"A meal is often associated with worship. Why? It is a way of confirming a covenant that has previously been cut. In the suzerain covenants, the soon-to-die suzerain would gather all of his followers together at a special ceremony involving a sacred meal. He would require them to pledge an oath of allegiance to his successor. Then, after he died, the successor would have another ceremony and meal. The followers would again pledge an oath and renew their covenant to seal legally and ritually the transfer of power. In Deuteronomy and Joshua the same process takes place. Israel is confirmed in its allegiance to Joshua with Moses. After the death of Moses, they have other ceremonies and meals to renew their covenant with their new leader (Josh. 5:10; 8:30-35). The confirmation of communion is supposed to be an ongoing process." [68]

Passover was the feast of the great meal with God. Following the

---

[68] **THAT YOU MAY PROSPER** I Ray Sutton I Institute for Christian Economics I June 1987 I Page 105 - 106

Suzerainty pattern, on that day, God offered Himself to whoever would have Him as Spouse and join His family. He called the family as a nation and as individuals. Those who would betroth themselves to Him sat down to a feast which gave life. The blood of the lamb was put on the threshold of the house, indicating that a marital covenant had been made between those in the house and the One Who would lead them to a new life with Himself.

"Ancient marriage customs often included the bride stepping over the threshold of her own volition, after the blood sacrifice. Still other customs involved not only the threshold but the lintel and doorposts as well. For example:

...on reaching her husband's house [a bride] is lifted up so that she can press against the door-lintel a piece of dough...The open hand of the bride stamps the dough as it is fixed in place, and in some cases the finger points are pricked before the stamping, so that the blood will appear as a sign...

Today's custom of the bridegroom carrying his bride over the threshold of the home they would share together is a vestige of the ancient one, as is tossing rice on the couple as they leave the wedding reception to begin their new life together.

It has been understood throughout ancient times that since the threshold was considered a sacred primitive altar, the doorway itself—lintel and doorposts—was looked upon as a framework over the altar fitting to bear tokens or inscriptions testifying to the sacredness of the place and the home as a sanctuary. The current Jewish custom of hanging a mezuzah on the front doorpost of the home is a remnant of the older

Hebrew custom when God's people were commanded by God to dedicate their doorways to Him (i.e., enter into a threshold covenant with God)." [69]

I hope you easily make the connection between this part of the marriage covenant and the Eucharist, which is the feast superlative of the Christian faith. The Eucharist is the meal of the covenant, but unlike the wedding meal, it goes further. It is also the nuptial chamber where union takes place and the two become one flesh. For the newly wed and the newly baptized, this union is real and substantive. And this is precisely where we part ways with Calvinists, Fundamentalists, and all others who deny that the Eucharist is the very Body and Blood of our Lord which was upon the Cross of Calvary. Every possible analogy of marriage and the nuptial bed is broken by their denial. This problem comes from the Reformers insistence of treating the covenant of our Lord as a Suzerainty treaty/contract rather than a marriage covenant in which the two become one flesh.

"The traditional Reformed or Calvinistic view of the sacraments, I contend, is the Biblical view. Like the Biblical view of Christ's historic kingdom authority, it is covenantal. It is therefore a representative view. In the sacraments, Christ is spiritually present, not or bodily present, and something really happens in history. The covenant has meaning and influence in history. Its sacraments change history because they are effectual. They are not mere symbols. Christ attains special presence through the representative meal of His people. The Biblical view therefore abandons both realism and nominalism. It

---

[69] **Life in Covenant I Covenant as Nuptial Communion I Fall 2012 I Nancy Jones** I www. http://lifeincovenant.com/?p=197#_ftn47

is instead a covenantal view." [70]

Bishop Sutton's idea is not the biblical idea. As I have taken pains to show, the biblical idea has to do with marriage, unity, and love. Sutton's Calvinism fits in perfectly with the idea of a contract, not a marriage. In contract making, one can send a representative. When I purchased my house from Mrs. Lillian King over 50 years ago, I did not deal directly with her. I dealt with her son as her representative. I never saw Mrs. King and had nothing to do with her. Why? Because there was no sense of a personal, intimate, loving relationship involved in what we were doing. It was a contract. I wanted something that she had, not her.

Try that with marriage. Try sending a representative to marry your spouse and see just how long the relationship lasts the minute the representative walks in the church and announces this intention. Representatives work for contracts. They have no place in a personal and intimate relationship.

We as bride have crossed the threshold into the kingdom home of the Son. We vow to be faithful to all that we have promised before entering the waters of baptism. As in earthly marriage, all that now remains is the consummation of the marriage through becoming one flesh.

This is where the Real Presence in the Eucharist is so important. Our Lord is not a spirit being. He is a man of real flesh and blood. If the marital covenant, with all that it points to, is a shadow and type of the reality of heaven, then in some way beyond our knowledge, we are going to experience a deep and joyful union with our divine Bridegroom. And we are going to experience it *flesh to flesh*, since both He and we shall be in glorified, resurrected fleshly bodies. This is why it is important to understand that we are not the vassal slaves that

---

[70] **THAT YOU MAY PROSPER** I Ray Sutton I **Institute for Christian Economics** I **June 1987** I **Page 312-313.**

Calvinist anthropology makes of us. We are bride to our divine Bridegroom. This presupposes a far more intimate relationship between us and Christ than that of rebellious serfs who are legally forgiven. Sutton and Calvinism entirely miss this point. In some way unknown to us, we will enter into an intensely joyful, extremely intimate, and beautiful union which is symbolized here on earth by the nuptial bed. Look at how beautifully Peter Kreeft expresses this reality:

"Since there are bodies in Heaven, able to eat and be touched, like Christ's resurrection body, there is the possibility of physical intercourse. But why might the possibility be actualized? What are its possible purposes and meanings?

We know Heaven by earthly clues. Let us try to read all the clues in earthly intercourse. It has three levels of meaning: the subhuman, or animal; the superhuman, or divine; and the specifically human. (All three levels exist in us humans.)

Animal reasons for intercourse include (1) the conscious drive for pleasure and (2) the unconscious drive to perpetuate the species. Both would be absent in Heaven. For although there are unimaginably great pleasures in Heaven, we are not driven by them. And the species is complete in eternity: no need for breeding.

Transhuman reasons for intercourse include (1) idolatrous love of the beloved as a substitute for God and (2) the Dante-Beatrice love of the beloved as an image of God. As to the first, there is, of course, no idolatry in Heaven. No substitutes for God are even tempting when God Himself is present. As to the second, the earthly beloved was a window to God, a mirror reflecting the divine beauty. That is why the lover was so smitten. Now that the reality is present, why stare at the mirror? The impulse to adore has found its perfect object. Furthermore, even on earth this love leads not to intercourse but to infatuation. Dante neither desired nor enacted intercourse with Beatrice.

Specifically human reasons for intercourse include (1) consummating

120

a monogamous marriage and (2) the desire to express personal love. As to the first, there is no marriage in Heaven. But what of the second?

I think there will probably be millions of more adequate ways to express love than the clumsy ecstasy of fitting two bodies together like pieces of a jigsaw puzzle. Even the most satisfying earthly intercourse between spouses cannot perfectly express all their love. If the possibility of intercourse in Heaven is not actualized, it is only for the same reason earthly lovers do not eat candy during intercourse: there is something much better to do. The question of intercourse in Heaven is like the child's question whether you can eat candy during intercourse: a funny question only from the adult's point of view. Candy is one of children's greatest pleasures; how can they conceive a pleasure so intense that it renders candy irrelevant? Only if you know both can you compare two things, and all those who have tasted both the delights of physical intercourse with the earthly beloved and the delights of spiritual intercourse with God testify that there is simply no comparison." [71]

I hope you see what Kreeft is getting at here. We think of intercourse in terms of genital sex. What goes on in heaven involves our bodies, but it goes far beyond such a thing because heaven is that far beyond earth. Yet nonetheless, it will in some fashion involve *a real uniting of us*, our whole beings, our energies, passions, souls, and everything that we are. Our union on earth is just a foretaste of intimacy and joy unimaginable.

Our Lord longs for this union with us even now. He is an impatient Lover of our souls. Therefore, the Eucharist is this eschaton reality being made actually present in time and space. Since there is no longer a separation between us because of the work of the Cross on our behalf, we can now, in a limited way

---

[71] Peter Kreeft | Will There Be Sex in Heaven? | From the book Everything You Ever Wanted to Know About Heaven but Never Dreamed of Asking | Ignatius Press | June 1, 1990.

because of our flesh and its limitations, experience the unitive love which comes from being "in Christ" and have Him in us. His Flesh and Blood, the energies of these divine components, and everything that is of Him, enters into us to unite with us in the temple of our souls. This is why many of the saints, upon receiving the Eucharist, went into ecstasy. They were experiencing the reality of heaven here and now, the reality of being truly made one flesh with Jesus as His Flesh entered them and He substantially united with them.

When a man takes his bride nuptially on the wedding night, the very essence of his life enters into her. Joined to the potential life within her, this union brings forth a new life which is a combination of the life essence of the two A similar thing happens to us as sinners when we receive the very life of God, the Blessed Eucharist, into our bodies. A new life is brought forth. St. Paul describes it in this fashion:

Eph 4: 24 And that ye put on *the new man*, which after God is created in righteousness and true holiness.

Col 3: 10 And have put on *the new [man]*, which is renewed in knowledge after the image of him that created him:

What is the "new man?" It is the life of Christ/God Himself entering into us, joining with our life, and creating a new being which is to inherit the kingdom of God and share in the divine nature. [72] Think of this amazing statement – we actually partake of the very nature of God Himself! Astounding!

That divine nature within us is the source of the new man which is created in holiness and righteousness. This involves a substantive change in the person I am as a sinner. I am no longer alive to sin but dead to it. I now have a new nature which lives to please my Father. This is a real change which makes

---

[72] **II Peter 1: 4**

me ontologically different than what I was. No paper declaration in heaven, no forensic justification can do this. We are not covered by the legal righteousness of Christ under which we still remain unchanged and the same, but we are made over. The reception of His life into us creates a new life in us. We are indeed infused with life and not just declared righteous.

This wonderful new life within us needs to be fed. Another familial term used in the Bible is that of babies. As a baby will die if left unfed, so our souls will die in the sense of never maturing on earth unless we receive the Bread of Life. Jesus said that He is the true bread come down from heaven. There is a new life within, made in the image of God.

This is not a fantasy. This life of the new man within has energy and force to it. It needs to be fed. You would not feed your child with readings from a cookbook. Knowing about the preparation of meals may satisfy some intellectual hunger, but it will not feed the body, which needs food to enter into it, nourish it, and give it life energy. Readings from the Bible will give us instruction and guidance, but they do not feed the divine life force which lives inside us. Our new man needs that which he can feed upon – the true Bread of Life. When Jesus enters my body through the Eucharist, He brings to me and shares with me the life force of His divine nature, so that I am fed and renewed.

We eat that which is living. Our food has life in it. This is why mankind cannot sustain life by eating inanimate objects. The life energy of what we eat is transferred to us so that we live and grow. When I take Jesus into my body, I take in Life which shares Himself with me so that I become a partaker of Life. Since the life I am receiving is the divine nature itself, the reception of the Eucharist is intended to make me become more and more like Jesus by the joining of my nature to His. This is a real ontological change, not a legal declaration of "imputed righteousness."

What I find odd is the denial of Christian history by Calvinists. Here are two famous quotes which go back to the Early church, showing that the Eucharist was believed as being the very Body and Blood of Christ:

"They [the Gnostics] abstain from the Eucharist and from prayer, because they confess not the Eucharist to be the flesh of our Saviour Jesus Christ, which suffered for our sins, and which the Father, of His goodness, raised up again. Those, therefore, who speak against this gift of God, incur death in the midst of their disputes. But it were better for them to treat it with respect, that they also might rise again. It is fitting, therefore, that ye should keep aloof from such persons, and not to speak of them either in private or in public, but to give heed to the prophets, and above all, to the Gospel, in which the passion [of Christ] has been revealed to us, and the resurrection has been fully proved. But avoid all divisions, as the beginning of evils." [73]

Justin Martyr clearly shows that from the beginning, the Church held that not only was the Eucharist the Flesh and Blood of Christ, it also wasn't bread and wine after the consecration. Here is Chapter 66 of his First Apology:

"And this food is called among us [the Eucharist], of which no one is allowed to partake but the man who believes that the things which we teach are true, and who has been washed with the washing that is for the remission of sins, and unto regeneration, and who is so living as Christ has enjoined. For not as common bread and common drink do we receive these; but in like manner as Jesus Christ our Saviour, having been made flesh by the Word of God, had both flesh and blood for our salvation, so likewise have we been taught that the food which is blessed by the prayer of His word, and from which our blood and flesh by transmutation are nourished, is the flesh and blood of that Jesus who was made flesh."

---

[73] **Ignatius of Antioch c. 103-107 A.D. | Letter to the Smyrnaeans, Chapter 7**

So once a certain prayer of His word is said, the bread and wine cease to be common bread and wine, and become spiritual Bread and Wine: namely, the Flesh and Blood of that Jesus Who was made Flesh. The prayer of His word is the prayer of consecration, as Justin explains, quoting Christ at the Last Supper. What's translated there as transmutation is incredible. The actual phrase is "kata metabolen," and that metabolen is the root word of our word "metabolize." What Justin is actually saying is that by the Eucharist, our own body and blood is nourish and metabolized by Christ. Just as when we eat bread and drink wine, we turn the elements into our body through metabolism, when we eat the Eucharist, Christ metabolizes us (so to speak) into His Body. This is very much consistent with the view scripture presents in places like 1 Corinthians 10:17. [74]

I find it fascinating, and profoundly sad, that a man as brilliant as Ray Sutton can allow anti-Catholic sentiment to so blind him to such clear reality.

SUMMARY

Imagine a newly married couple who would retire to the privacy of their honeymoon suite, take out their marriage certificate, and spend the night looking at it. Preposterous! Yet that is exactly what the fascination with preaching is in Protestant assemblies. The written Word is merely the marriage certificate. The Eucharist is the nuptial bed, where that which has been united in covenant is sealed by becoming one flesh. It is the reality of the promise in the written Word.

Or as Flannery O'Connor more succinctly put it at a dinner party in New York City one night: "If it's just a symbol, then the hell with it."

---

[74] Joe Heschmeyer | Shameless Popery | Very Early Church Fathers on the Eucharist | http://catholicdefense.blogspot.com/2010/11/early-church-fathers -on-eucharist.html

JUSTIFICATION: ENTERING INTO AND STAYING IN THE COVENANT FAMILY

As a Protestant, understanding Sutton's five principles of a Suzerainty treaty/covenant, and then applying them to the marital covenant which is expressed in Ezekiel 16:8 brought me to the threshold of the apostolic faith. I only needed a little bit more of an intellectual shove to get me in. That shove came in the form of Robert Sungenis' book, *Not by Faith Alone: A Biblical Study of the Catholic Doctrine of Justification.* This is no simple tract of a few pages, a drive-by shooting at the Protestant teaching on justification. It is an eight hundred page tome; a systematic destruction of a false sixteenth century doctrinal invention called "forensic justification."

The Sacraments of Confession and the Eucharist are at the heart of our justification before God. In order to understand the necessity of the Body and Blood of Christ being truly present in the Eucharist, it is necessary to discuss and destroy the myth which started the Reformation, that of forensic justification or imputed righteousness.

The issue again comes down to the difference between a legal contract and a family covenant. There is a great conflict between the adherents of forensic (imputed) justification and experienced (infused) justification. This conflict has spilled over into the arena of the covenant; therefore, it must be dealt with. You see, there is an idea floating about which discusses the covenant in terms of declarative (forensic) justification. Here is another lengthy passage from Bishop Sutton's book:

"Romans 3:24 Being justified [legally declared right with God] by his grace through the redemption that is in Christ Jesus: 25 Whom God hath set forth to be a propitiation [payment] through faith in his blood, to declare his righteousness for the remission of sins that are past, through the forbearance of God; 26 To declare, I say, at this time his righteousness: that he might be just, and the justifier of him which believeth in Jesus. 27 Where is boasting then? It is excluded. By what law? of works? Nay: but by the law of faith. 28 Therefore we conclude that a man is justified by faith without the deeds of the law.

Romans 4:5 But to him that worketh not, but believeth on him that justifieth the ungodly, his faith is counted [imputed] for righteousness.

When a man is saved, <u>righteousness is laid to his account,</u> and he is <u>declared</u> right, justified. This way, unregenerate men can have salvation. They do not have to become good before they can be saved. They cannot become good before they are saved. They are objectively saved because God declares them to be saved. They are objectively good because God <u>declares</u> them to be objectively good. He can do this in terms of His covenant because of Christ's objective work *of salvation in history. <u>That objective work is imputed to the redeemed person by God's grace</u>. In theology, this is often described as the objective side of salvation. Always, the objective forms the basis of the subjective. Normally, the term "objective" is applied to salvation, but this redemptive concept pulls over into all of life, making every relationship <u>grounded in the legal or objective</u>. That which is declared legal by God is therefore objectively legal." [75]*

Notice that despite Bible passages which speak of Old Testament figures such as Abel as being righteous men, Sutton insists that men cannot become good before they are saved. The above passage is the mantra of Calvinists. Said often enough and loudly enough, one actually could begin to believe that this is what St Paul meant when he wrote the book of Romans and spoke of imputed righteousness. Nothing could be further from the truth. I find it odd that men who have a high degree of education, with the ability to read the scriptures in Greek, will somehow ignore the meaning of the Greek word which is translated "imputed" and instead imprint their own meaning upon it.

In the Bible, the English word "imputed" is the Greek word *logizomai*. In three different Protestant publications, Vine's Bible Dictionary, Kittle's Theological Dictionary of the NT, and Strong's Concordance, it is described as an accounting term. It is the same word used of those who count money and should be used in the same way, that the one imputing is actually counting what is really there. In no sense does it mean that one counts what another has and imputes it to the bankrupt account, claiming that the bankrupt one is suddenly flush with money that is not really there. In no sense does it mean to deal with anything other than reality. Look at the definition box I have posted below from Strong's Concordance at Blue Letter Bible online, a distinctly Protestant website:

[75] **THAT YOU MAY PROSPER** I Ray Sutton I Institute for Christian Economics I June 1987 I Page 29.

128

> "This word deals with reality. If I reckon (logizomai) that my bank book has $25 in it, it has $25 in it. ***Otherwise I am deceiving myself.*** This word refers more to *fact* than supposition or opinion."

Yet this is exactly what Protestants think that God does when dealing with mankind, He deceives Himself as to our true condition, and as Luther said, hides us under a snow-white blanket of Christ's righteousness. Not according to the Protestant Strong's Lexicon!

Romans 4:21 And being fully persuaded that, what he had promised, he was able also to perform. 22 And therefore it was imputed to him for righteousness 23 Now it was not written for his sake alone, that it was imputed to him: 24 But for us also, to whom it shall be imputed, if we believe on him that raised up Jesus our Lord from the dead;

These verses from Romans are the absolute favorite of Calvinists to proof-text as a way of saying that our works do nothing for us and the only way we are seen as righteous by God is for Him to "impute" (i.e. lend to us) the righteousness of Christ so that we might be seen in His eyes as righteous. Calvinists say that Abraham believed God and therefore, since Abraham believed God, God gave him a righteousness which was not intrinsic to Abraham himself. This is the basis of imputation, which says that we, by believing in Christ, receive Christ's righteousness as a covering for ourselves, since in ourselves we are nothing but dunghills in God's sight.

There's a real problem with this view. Not only does the Greek not support it, but there is another Bible verse that torpedoes and sinks this idea.

1 John 3:7 Little children, let no man deceive you: he that doeth righteousness is righteous, even as he is righteous.

St. John does not describe righteousness using the wording of imputation. He is very clear to state that he who *does* (notice the emphasis on "doing" or works) righteousness is righteous.

Heb 11:33 Who through faith subdued kingdoms, wrought righteousness, obtained promises, stopped the mouths of lions,

How could the OT saints have "wrought righteousness" without the indwelling of the Holy Spirit and the doctrine of imputation?

Romans 4:13 For the promise, that he should be the heir of the world, was not to Abraham, or to his seed, through the law, but through the righteousness of faith.

The righteousness of faith. You see, faith is righteous. Having faith in God is a righteous act, and the more faith we have, the more righteous we are being. Great faith, as shown by our works, means that we are greatly righteous. Conversely, without faith, we have no intrinsic righteousness. Abraham was truly righteous. He did not need an alien righteousness imputed to his account. God saw a righteous man and counted it as such.

Ro 4:9 Cometh this blessedness then upon the circumcision only, or upon the uncircumcision also? for we say that faith was *reckoned* to Abraham for righteousness.

Faith is reckoned (or counted) as righteousness. The word here for reckoned is once again "logizomai", which means to count what is really there. When God sees faith, He sees righteousness.

This Calvinist idea of being right with God is also called "forensic justification." The meaning of this little phrase is pretty much the same as imputed righteousness. It means that a man, by the force of faith alone is given a real and *legal status* of being justified before God that will never be taken away from him. Foundational to this belief is the idea that men, being dead in sins, simply can do no righteous thing on their own. Therefore, to be justified, all men and women born from Adam must have a legal declaration of righteousness because they have no righteousness of their own upon which to fall. Yet as I studied the book of 1 John one morning, I came upon this interesting verse.

1 John 3:12 Not as Cain, who was of that wicked one, and slew his brother. And wherefore slew he him? Because his own works were evil, and his brother's righteous.

So here is Abel, doing an act of sacrifice and the Lord says, by the pen of divine inspiration, that his works were *righteous*! It does not say that Abel was given an alien righteousness. It says clearly that Abel's works were righteous. In light of the Calvinist idea that man is a stinking, rotten corpse who can do no good before God, this is verse shows Calvinism's idea of imputation of righteousness to be false.

God set forth a choice before Cain and Abel. He even called to Cain and urged Cain to be an obedient covenant child. This is strange behavior on God's part if He, being omniscient, knows that both of these boys are dead in their sins and unable to respond at all.

At this point, rather than take the Word of God at face value, in order to keep their theological novums in place, Calvinists will insist that Abel was one of the elect of God and Cain was not. Thus Abel was given the ability to have faith from an outside source in order to obey God and Cain was not. But this idea only gets one into deeper and more murky water, since the Holy Spirit had not been given at that time to, *"live inside of men and enable them to obey the Law of God."* [76] He was, according to all the teachings I have heard from both Evangelicals and Calvinists, the One Who came upon men for certain services unto God, but did not actually live in man as the temple of God. Therefore, we must insist that Cain and Abel were both externally entreated to do right by the Holy Spirit and made their decisions on the basis of their own wills.

Abel, acting with faith in what God said, performs an act of obedience, believing in God's word to him. This is a righteous act, and God sees and recorded it as such in the scriptures for all time. Thus, for all time Abel is called righteous because he did a righteous deed, not because he was imputed some foreign righteousness which was not an intrinsic part of who he was.

After our salvation, the Eucharist comes into play. Sutton pleads the Protestant understanding; that we can only be righteous by being declared to be righteous. This leaves us unchanged and untouched internally. This is the only way that Calvinists can think of justification and righteousness because it supports the first principle of Calvinists belief, which is Total Depravity. If we are totally depraved, then even after salvation, we cannot have true righteousness. Therefore, something must be added to us – a declaration of being righteous.

But can the very energies of Christ our God enter our bodies in the Eucharist, unite intimately with us in a way analogized by the nuptial bed, and leave us unchanged? Are you kidding me? Does the Jesus enter into a man and insulate Himself into some compartment of a man's being, or does he unite Himself so intimately with a person as to distinctly affect what that person is in his core being? I must opt for the latter. It is not a legal declaration of change. It is a completely new ontological reality.

Our Orthodox understanding follows the familial pattern, for when a

---

[76] This is the Calvinist view, in which the indwelling of the Holy Spirit enables men to obey the law of God and thus be justified.

132

man enters his spouse, there is a real and substantial change within. Modern medical technology is constantly discovering a myriad of interesting facts about the human body. One recent discovery is that during lovemaking, a woman's body secretes a hormone which makes her psychologically bond with her mate. This works even for women who are having sex with a random male, and is thought to be a reason many women stay in abusive relationships for years.

More than that, of course, is when the life force of the man meets the life force of the woman and a new life is created. Talk about a serious ontological change! How much more do the energies of Christ enter into us in the Eucharist and both create and support what the Apostle Paul called "the new man, created in righteousness." [77] This new life in us is also righteous because it is the union of ourselves with Christ. It does not need to be hidden under a legal declaration of righteousness which covers us from God's wrath.

Of even more concern, I must ask if God can call that which is intrinsically evil to be good? Did God declare the Creation to be good and then it became good (implying that it was either neutral, or worse, evil, before such declaration), or did God declare that which was already fact? When He said of Noah that he saw Noah a righteous man in a wicked generation, was God declaring that which existed, or was He making Noah righteous by declaration?

God, Who is Truth, does not declare a thing to be that which it is not. He does not have to declare us good by a legal fiat because as part of His Creation, we are good! But more than that, as I have shown elsewhere, it is possible for one to be righteous, yet not in the Body of Christ. Such was the case with a host of people in the OT who lived before the indwelling of the Holy Spirit. This is why the Church allows that there are those who are "unwitting law keepers" who, in keeping with Romans 2: 13-16, keep the law of God's love placed in

---

[77] Ephesians 4:24 And that ye put on the new man, which after God is created in righteousness and true holiness.

their hearts by the Holy Spirit. God sees them also as righteous. Righteousness is not a legal declaration, it is a state of being. He does not use legal language to cover up our failures. He deals with reality.

Does this mean that we can save ourselves? Certainly not. If you are asking this question, you have not understood the chapter I wrote on salvation and I would ask you to go back and read it again. Christ alone saves mankind by establishing a covenant into which we can enter. The Bible states that Abel, Noah, Abraham, and others were righteous, but their righteousness was insufficient to establish the New Covenant to redeem mankind, save themselves, and create a New Covenant with the Father. To redeem mankind, it took the perfect righteousness of Christ so that He, as Last Adam, could do that which Adam failed to do. Our righteousness, which is the righteousness of faith according to scripture, responds to the overtures of Christ and enters covenant with Him.

Calvinists don't believe we are capable of this, claiming that man is totally depraved, a term neither found in the Bible nor, as I have shown earlier, supported by it. I do not wish to come to God for salvation and depend upon anything I can do or offer as a means to earn my way into the covenant family. Outside of the covenant, I am not part of God's covenant family, the Church, nor am I one who has anything of worth to God by which I could earn forgiveness and salvation. But in the covenant family, through baptism I have been adopted, I am called a beloved child, and as I keep covenant, God deals with me as a child, which is to say that He can deal with me in grace and not by the Law. Calvinists may speak of a covenant of grace, but they do not understand what they are saying, for they treat our salvation as law court and law-keeping, rather than family and the actions of a loving Father.

Heb 9:16 For where a testament is, there must also of necessity be the death of the testator. 17 For a testament is of force after men are

134

dead: otherwise it is of no strength at all while the testator liveth.

Christ did just this as the perfect man. When we cut covenant with Him through baptism, we enter the one and only eternal covenant by becoming His eternal Spouse. Just as Christ belongs to the Father, by being espoused to Christ, we also belong to the Father. God can now deal with us according to mercy instead of bare justice because we are in the covenant and are relationally in Christ. All that Christ has is ours, including righteousness, but it is not a righteousness that is imputed to us. There is a difference between being intrinsically unrighteous, filthy, totally depraved dung hills hidden under a cloak of Christ's righteousness and being righteousness because we are ontologically changed and brought into right relationship with God through Christ.

Bishop Sutton and Calvinists further strive to make biblical their Reformed understanding of the elect by claiming that when one falls away from the faith, that one was never a believer (aka "of the elect") in the first place. I think Protestants are scared to accept that a man may become righteous by uniting to Christ and then have the freedom to walk away from that union. It seems to cast God in the position of being an Indian giver. However, it is not God who is unfaithful, it is us.

Have not you yourself said, Bishop Sutton, we can expect the blessings of the covenant *"only as long as we remain faithful to that covenant?"* [78]

How does Sutton with a straight face claim to be covenantal in his understanding of salvation and at the same time present a soteriology which denies that man may break his covenant with Christ and leave that covenant relationship? Why take the position of those who deny this covenant principle

---

[78]

"Since God and man do not have unity of being, God dictates the terms (commandments) under which man can have a relation-ship with Him. These terms are the standard of the covenant. Man is called to be faithful to God by submitting to them. If he submits (covenant-keeping), he is blessed. If he does not, (covenant-breaking) he is cursed."

by their insistence that man is made righteous by a permanent legal decree which cannot be lost? That is not covenant. Covenants are conditional, based on the keeping or breaking of the oaths/sanctions, and therefore, as with all relationships, can be broken. And as with the family, we can lose our inheritance if we walk away from it.

The Parable of the Prodigal Son is a tremendous illustration of this. When I was a Fundamentalist, I heard this parable described as a sinner getting saved. Nonsense. Whoever teaches this is not paying close attention to the parable and the typology. The Prodigal is already a son! He is not a stranger seeking adoption into the family at the end of the narrative. He is family. This is a picture of the believer who has a relationship with his Father. We are in the family covenant I have spoken of in previous chapters. The Prodigal Son is already in the family in the parable, just as after our entrance into the covenant family through baptism, we are part of the family.

The boy goes to his father and deeply insults him. Then he leaves. This is the equivalent of a sin which not only severs the relationship with our Father, but in most cases, drives us out of the household and into the wilderness of sinful pleasures. We trade the Father's love, and the household of God, for the pigsty of sin.

In the parable, the boy believes he will come to be his true self by being separated from his father. Yet he finds that the riches of his father do not go into the far land of sin with him. This is a perfect picture of how we as creatures attempt to find our true selves outside of a living and vital relationship with our divine Spouse. The reality of our true selves is found in relationship with God and His sharing everything He has within a family relationship. Outside that relationship, there is the bareness of the "no-life" without the Father's love.

In the parable, the boy comes to his senses and returns. He does the same thing that we do upon returning. He confesses his covenant breaking(Sacrament of Repentance), he is restored by his father (ring and clothing, signifying the restoration of covenant and all authority with it), and then they eat the covenant meal of restoration (Sacrament of Eucharist). All is right again and the boy is once again in line for the father's inheritance. (Come on, you don't really believe Dad gave him everything he had, do you?)

But what if he had not returned? What if he had not come to his senses and had died in the pigsty? Would he have received the inheritance? Please follow the analogy. No! Even though never stopped being a son and the covenant of blood between them was still in his veins, he would have received nothing. We also will receive none of the promised covenant blessings if we break the covenant we entered into and turn from the Father and His family, the Church. There is no idea expressed in the Parable of the Prodigal Son which says "Oh, well, he was never a son in the first place. We see that by his behavior." There are four distinct places in the NT where we see the Judgment Seat of Christ and see the wicked and the righteous gathered together: Matthew 25: 31-46, John 5: 28-29, Romans 2:5-10 and Revelation 20: 11-15. This is the Last Judgment. Many people I have spoken with have insisted that these verses are not the Last Judgment, but rather are the Great White Throne, where only unbelievers are judged and condemned. The problem with this idea is that once again, scripture does not allow for such an idea. In each section of verses, the good and the bad are raised at the same time, gathered together, and separated according to their works. There is no idea at all of a so-called Bema Seat Judgment of Christ, and from everything I read online defending this idea, it is made up of whole cloth in order to support the unscriptural idea that Christ's death on the Cross paid for all sins, past, present, and future, so that the only judgment which comes upon the believer is the degree of reward he will receive.

It is amazing how one error leads to another and then another and then another. This is because if Protestants admitted that there is no such thing as "forensic justification," the whole soteriological house of cards they have so carefully constructed over the centuries would utterly collapse.

Let's look at one of the sections I have mentioned. Faith is not a one-time legal declaration of innocence. It is the first of a series of works in a process of salvation, a journey which will lead us to be judged by our works, according to Romans 2: 6-11:

Romans 2:6 Who will render to every man according to his deeds: 7 To them who by patient continuance in well doing seek for glory and honor and immortality, eternal life: 8 But unto them that are contentious, and do not obey the truth, but obey unrighteousness, indignation and wrath, 9 Tribulation and anguish, upon every soul of man that doeth evil, of the Jew first, and also of the Gentile; 10 But glory, honour, and peace, to every man that worketh good, to the Jew first, and also to the Gentile: 11 For there is no respect of persons with God.

Notice first of all that it is every man. This is neither a judgment seat of believers only unto reward, nor a judgment seat of unbelievers only unto condemnation. The good and the bad are gathered together. Every means every, good and bad alike, all mankind that has lived for all of time on earth!

Notice also that the judgment rendered to each is done according to his deeds, not according to some mythological idea of faith alone which was cooked up by the Protestant Reformation. There is, in fact, no mention at all of faith here. It is the deeds that men have done that determines their destiny. Works are faith in action. Works are also the process by which we keep the covenant oaths we made upon entering the Church.

Verse seven begins the process of separation by speaking of a class of men who by patient continuance in well doing (i.e. good works!) seek for glory and honor and immortality, eternal life. How does a person possibly read this verse and insist that this is somehow about the believer who is already saved getting his crowns of reward? This is about the family inheritance – which is life.

The next verse talks of the other class of men who will appear before Christ on the Judgment Day. Those wicked who did not obey the truth, who were contentious and did evil.

There is simply no indication in these verses that Christ sits in judgement and fools Himself as to the condition of the man or woman before Him. He deals with us for what we have actually been. This understanding is in line with James when he says that we are justified by our works.

This section of Romans by itself absolutely destroys the idea of imputed righteousness for if this is true, how do people who are seen as good by being in Christ even need to stand before Him to be judged for the reception of eternal life? If in the forensic model, all we must do is die and we are seen perfect, why are we warned of this Eschaton Judgement where our works are either covenantally judged to receive reward or curse? Forensic justification makes this judgment an exercise in silliness.

What this shows is the Elder Son (Christ) of the Father's family administering covenant blessing and curse. To those who have been faithful covenant keepers, the inheritance of life. To those who either spurned membership in the family, or, having been in the family, returned to the pigsties of sin, disinheritance. Why judge someone as to whether or not they have been a faithful covenant keeper if they are guaranteed to enter heaven anyway by their mere declaration of mental assent to a bunch of ideas?

Called as sons, we enter into the kingdom family by the adoption of grace, which takes place in our baptism. If at baptism we are imputed righteousness and stand as fully justified before God, why are we called in scripture to theosis, or becoming like Christ? Forensic justification is a declaration that we are already like Christ in God's eyes, for He sees not us, but Christ. If a declaration of justification gives us the perfect righteousness of Christ, then why are we called to grow in holiness? If declarative justification makes us really perfect, where are all the saints in time who suddenly one day were objectively as perfect as Christ upon this earth?

I have to keep reminding myself that this understanding comes because the Reformers treated the covenant like a legal contract. In it, they state that Christ kept the covenant with God perfectly for us, so that when we are in Him as the elect, we are no longer under the threat of condemnation because Christ has kept all points of righteousness for us.

Do you see the problem here? In a covenant, as I have said before, which bears repeating, no one can make a covenant for another! I cannot stress that strongly enough. Christ cannot do for us the good works which are the basis of covenant faithfulness. We must, according to the verses which speak of the Last Judgment, do them ourselves and have them to present to Him at the Judgment! No man can marry a woman on behalf of another man. Impossible!

This confusion comes, as I have said, by seeing the New Covenant of our Lord, which He makes with the Father for all mankind, to be the same as our individual covenant with Him. The first one, Christ does by Himself, without our help, and for us entirely. None of us could renew the eternal covenant and restore mankind to relationship with the Father.

Our covenant is different. We must make it with Christ to marry Him as our divine Spouse. Each one of us is responsible to take this action individually to be part of this new family which He has established. And then, at the end of our lives, we are judged as to whether or not we have been faithful covenant keepers by what we have done. It is the difference between redemption, salvation, and eternal life, three entirely different actions which the Reformers have completely mixed together, and in doing so, have confused everyone. But even worse than the confusion is the fact that in following this confused soteriology, men have been induced to wicked behavior.

If our righteousness is merely declarative, we then can have a supposed righteousness which is totally separated from a vigorous and living unity with our Lord, expressing itself in a life of good works. This is the whole basis of the "once saved – always saved" heresy in which a man may live a lukewarm and indifferent life on earth yet fully expect that he may obtain heaven because he has been declared righteous. It is said of Luther's Germany that once the peasants figured this out for themselves, they took it to the logical conclusion, which means that they turned Germany into a moral sewer of fornication. But why not? After all, if you are not depending upon your works and you are covered by a snow-white blanket of Christ's righteousness, then have at it!

In such a soteriological understanding, the believer need never again consider the state of his soul from day to day, for he has been once and for all justified. As such, he has no need of living out the life of Christ within the Church and through a vibrant connection to the Sacraments. Since justification is merely heavenly paperwork, so to speak, then there is no need of the Sacramental life to confer the grace of God. What point then my works, especially the Sacraments?

I cannot begin to count the numbers of people with whom I have talked who, as a logical outcome of this thinking, have told me point blank that they do not need to be a member of the Church in order to be a Christian. My response would be to remind them of the saying of St. Cyprian:

"He who will not have the Church as his mother will not have God as his Father."

On the great Day of God's Judgement, there are going to be a lot of people horribly surprised to find that they have been disinherited by a rebellion of their own choosing. The historic apostolic faith never taught such an idea of the covenant. Such a covenant would be an unconditional covenant. Where in the Bible does God have an unconditional covenant, having no blessings for obedience and curse for disobedience? But this is exactly what I get from Protestants with whom I debate. There is no idea of covenant ethics, no idea of oaths/sanctions, and therefore, no real seen need to perform good works to keep one in good standing as a covenant keeper.

Even the covenant of Abraham was threatened as God almost killed Moses for not circumcising his son. In the oaths/sanctions parameter of the covenant which Bishop Sutton has discovered and written of, lies the very fact that the covenant is conditional, for an unconditional covenant would not have oaths and sanctions. Baptism is an oath, a promise of obedience to Christ. Eternal death is the sanction for disobedience to that oath. Salvation is unconditional and free unto all who will enter the covenant of God by baptism, but eternal life is conditional as the reward/inheritance of being faithful.

Finally, forensic justification destroys the need for the Sacraments. A covenant is a conditional relationship and can be broken by either side. God, being perfect and immutable, will never break His vows to us. Sadly, however, being only human and made of dust, we all too frequently violate our covenant vows. There are times that we even completely sever our covenant relationship with our divine Bridegroom.

When a relationship is strained or severed, it must be renewed. We must come to a point of of right relationship again. Sincere repentance, apologies, and forgiveness precede the restoration of a broken relationship. Sometimes the offense is so great that the parties part and the covenant is left behind, broken and unrepaired. Think of the wife who, after enduring years of her husband's philandering and lies to her, decides that she will no longer forgive him, and files for divorce, making final and legal that which has already happened in their hearts. They are no longer one, and the relationship is finished.

We are blessed with the most loving, the most longsuffering, and the most forgiving of Spouses. Our divine Spouse will never break His covenant vows to us. More wonderfully, He stands always ready to forgive and restore us to Himself if we are repentant. A man or woman who leaves Jesus does so because they have found another lover (sin) which they do not wish to give up.

142

As long as we are able to repent and return, our Lord will forgive and receive us back into our covenant relationship, no matter how egregious our failure to love. But just as the covenant was originally entered into by means of a blood sacrifice, so the renewal of the covenant must also be made in the same way. If we have sinned a sin worthy of death, then a life must be given. That is the symbolism of the shedding of blood in the making of a covenant. Covenant is the giving of life sacrificially to another. Marriage in Orthodoxy is a beautiful representation of this, since the Crowning Ceremony is considered an entrance into martyrdom.[79] Blood represents that life and the shedding of blood represents the sacrifice. When I walk away from God, I have literally made an act of covenant with a false spouse. There must be an act of giving my life again to my Lord, Who alone is my true spouse. Something sacrificial must be done, an act in which I offer a blood renewal of the covenant, since all covenants are made and renewed with blood (the offering of life.) My part is to offer my repentance and turning back to Christ. His part is the Blood of the Eucharist.

Forensic justification cannot renew the covenant we have broken because there is no sacrifice to be applied. Forensic justification is more based in the heresy of Gnosticism, which places a premium on things that are not physical. Thus, I have heard Protestants try to defend their heretical and non-sacrificial view of the Lord's Supper by saying *"the things of the flesh are of no profit. Jesus meant that spiritually."*

No, He didn't. He died in the flesh on the Cross. He was raised in the flesh in a new fleshly body. The physical – the flesh – is involved intimately in our salvation because it is an intimate and real part of who we are. The idea that

---

79

They are now joined as God intended man and woman to be joined together; giving themselves totally and freely to the other. The crowns also symbolize the crown of martyrdom or witnessing to Christ for the couple incarnates the love of Christ for the Church. They also represent the royal authority of the children of God.

God despises the use of the physical as part of our salvation is an ancient heresy called Gnosticism. Gnostics deny the Resurrection because the physical is of this evil world. The truly good in Gnosticism is the spiritual. The body is of no use in salvation and to a Gnostic, worthless. Which attitude I find rather odd, given the history of Gnostics. They have a well-deserved reputation as libertines and of being sexually immoral. Go figure!

SUMMARY

Because Luther could not see God as loving Father, but rather as severe and strict Judge, One Who demands absolute perfection, he could get no relief from the fears of God that tormented him. He was an easy target for the evil one and the doctrine of imputed righteousness which has no support in scripture whatsoever. The Law may demand perfection – a Father desires love. God is love, but Luther – and by extension many of the Calvinists I have met – could not see this. For the Calvinist mind, law-keeping is the totality of the Christian life. This goes back, as I said before, to seeing mankind not as sons and daughters in the covenant family, but as vassal slaves. Speaking as a father, I was never angry with my children when they tried to do right and did not do it perfectly. Luther's imagery of God is that father who can never be pleased, no matter how hard you try. Thus, knowing he could never be perfect, and therefore in his tortured mind never acceptable to God the Judge, Luther was in despair. Minds that are in a frenzy of despair are easy prey to fallacious ideas to relieve that agony.

FIVE PRINCIPLES OF A COVENANT FAMILY

Transcendence	The greater offers covenant to the lesser
Hierarchy	Who's in charge here?
Ethics	What are the rules?
Oaths/Sanctions	Promises by which relationship is maintained.
Succession	Continuation through the ages.

These are the five principles of a covenant, but if I have done anything of a good job in discussing covenant and family, you will realize that covenant is an intimate relationship which results in family. I hope in this chapter to show that the principles of a Suzerainty covenant/treaty which Calvinists believe make up our covenant can also define personal intimacy and family.

I found the acrostic THEOS to be most helpful in memorizing the principles in when I needed to bring them up in a discussion of the covenant. Let me see now if I can break these principles down and show how they support the Church as God's covenant family on earth.

Transcendence: In a covenant, the greater offers covenant and all of the blessings of that relationship to the lesser. In the family unit of the patriarchal world which God created, this means that the man has always been, or at least, should be, the one who offers his strength, protection, and blessings to the woman. In a masculine society, men are raised to be strong, warriors capable of protecting all under their covenant headship. This protection can be that of physically combating an aggressor force, either individually or as part of a standing body ready to protect the country in which his family lives. In times of peace, this protection can also be that of protection against hunger and privation by going to work every day. The world in which we live today is a far cry from that ideal. In this world, men have become predatory upon women though things such as pornography, institutionalizing abortion, rape, violence against women, and a host of other behaviors. The legion of single mothers who struggle to live every day is a mute testimony to the abandonment of this principle of covenant blessing and protection by men.

But how does this apply to the Church?

The Church is the great Kingdom of God on earth. It is visible to all and reaches out to all to offer an entrance into the covenant of God. In Suzerainty treaties as well as family relationships, the greater offers the protection of his might to the lesser. A proper marriage is entered into when a man (the greater) offers his protection, wealth, and blessing to a woman (the lesser). A true husband and father protects his wife and children, even, if necessary, at the cost of his own life. This familial pattern follows that of the Suzerain Great King offering vassal kings under his rule the protection of his army. The lesser is defended by the greater.

In like manner, the Church offers to all mankind certain protections for our own good. The Church is the transcendent authority on earth, above all man-made institutions, even those thousands of ecclesial bodies which have sprung up as a result of the Protestant rebellion against Rome.

146

The proof of this authority and protection from error is easy to find. Look at the institutions which are most frequently associated with the Protestant Reformation. Look at the peril which in which they place their members as they now teach that homosexual acts are acceptable, that abortion is morally permissible, that contraception and in vitro fertilization are allowable. The world cannot understand why the Church does not get with the times and allow the teaching of these and other morally repugnant and soul-destroying ideas. Yet it is because the Church, the transcendent protector of all in Her bosom, cannot do this. She belongs to Christ, and as His Bride, Christ will protect Her from teaching error.

Bishop Sutton says: *"Transcendence means the covenant is created by a legal declaration. As a result of this declaration, a certain legal status is imputed to the relationship. We can call this the doctrine of imputation, a legal term meaning "to apply to the account of."* [80]

No, Bishop Sutton. Not only is that not what the Greek word *"logizomai"* means, it is not how marriage is made. Marriage is made when two become one flesh. It is made by *union*, not legal decree. Remember when Jacob worked for seven years for Rachael, only to wake up the next morning and find that he was married to Leah? How is that possible? Because he united with her. He became one flesh with her. He had to work another seven years for Rachael.

If covenant is made by legal decree, then I could go to a courthouse, and if I found a judge corrupt enough to receive a large sum of cash, have a legal decree made out for a woman I want and go to her and say, "Guess what? We're married!" Even if our already crazy society became bizarre enough to accept such legality, would it really be a marriage in the sense of two giving themselves in sacrificial love to each other as an icon of the Trinity? When a man takes a

---

[80] **THAT YOU MAY PROSPER** I Ray Sutton I Institute for Christian Economics I June 1987 I Page 27.

woman by force, without either her desire or consent of will, we call it rape.

In Calvinism, our divine Bridegroom does not woo us to Himself and bring us into an intimate relationship based on our desire to unite in love with Him. The Calvinist view of salvation is this: man is dead. He cannot respond at all. God selects a certain number and brings them to life. They have no will about this, no choice to make, no personal input in the whole process at all. It is analogous to a man seeing a woman he likes and taking her by force and without her consent to be his wife. The whole Calvinist paradigm of salvation is at odds with the idea of the way love works. It is more like rape than marriage.

The Church is the embodiment of the transcendent God. Sutton and his cohorts deny this, but his own words and the Bible condemn him. In his book, he writes several paragraphs on what he calls false transcendence:

"Guess who becomes the god of this world if this creator god of deism is far, far away? You guessed it! Man does. Man becomes the substitute god. The creator god is "on vacation." He does not judge kings, kingdoms, or bureaucrats. When it comes to exercising judgment in history, he defaults. Man can speak; deism's god is silent. Man's word therefore substitutes for god's word. Man substitutes himself for this substitute god. Man becomes the god of the system, knowing (determining) good and evil." [81]

Is this not a perfect description of what the Reformers did? They rejected much which Christ taught the Apostles, including the authority that Christ gave them, and came up with their own interpretation of "thus saith the Lord" in the Bible. Now, thanks to this rejection of the transcendence of the Church over mankind, given by Christ Himself to the Apostles, we have literally hundreds of

---

[81]   **THAT YOU MAY PROSPER** I Ray Sutton I Institute for Christian Economics I June 1987 I Page 33.

148

competing assemblies, all claiming to teach God's truth and yet all in conflict
with each other. Rejecting the authority of the transcendent can only lead to such
chaos. Men have become their own determiners of truth, rather than listening to
God speak through His covenant Bride, the Church.[82]

If you look through Christian history, it is was the universal Church
which defended the great doctrines of the faith. Not the Roman Catholic Church,
the Western Church at Rome, but the united Church of East and West before the
lamentable schism of 1054 AD. The successors of the Apostles met in councils
to determine the mind of God and the truth of various teachings which sprung up.
Notice that every heresy, every teaching that we would reject as false, such as
Christ as created being (Arianism) comes from an individual doing exactly what
Sutton spoke of – becoming or desiring to become the god of the system. It is a
desire for self-transcendence and authority, the same sin which was found in
Satan. Rome did the same thing when the Frankish bishops inserted the Filoque
clause into the Creed, despite the concicular warnings and anathema pronounced
against anyone who would do this! This rebellion, this desire for false autonomy,
went right down the line as Rome experienced the Protestant Reformers doing
the same thing.

The familial model of this chaos would be a family of twelve children.
In this covenant structure, the family, the father teaches what is the acceptable
behavior which will maintain the unity of love. But the children, rather than
accepting his transcendent authority, begin to interpret his words differently and
begin to act in ways that are displeasing to him. Pretty soon you have chaos in
the family. The chores are not getting done, children are arguing and fighting
among themselves, and the whole thing is a terrible witness to the other families
in the neighborhood who are watching this.

The Church as family of God was given the chore of spreading the Good

---

[82] 1 Timothy 3:5; Matthew 18: 17; Matthew 16:18.

News to the world and inviting all outside the kingdom family to enter the covenant and experience the blessings therein. The Church is also given the task of disciplining those who enter Her, helping them to turn from evil and do good, to find deeper and more intimate relationship with Christ, and to ultimately inherit eternal life. Jesus said that our unity would be a sign that the Father had truly sent Him into the world.[83] What does disunity tell the watching world?

Think now of the average pagan in Africa who sees eight different missionaries from eight opposing theological viewpoints enter his village. Does he think that Christ was sent by the true God for the salvation of his soul? More likely he thinks that Christianity is a religion of half-baked dimwits and wants nothing to do with it!

Covenant transcendence is also closely linked with all the other principles of a covenant, including the next one.

Hierarchy: I am amazed that the men who accept this principle of covenant do not see what the Protestant Rebellion has done to God's authority on earth. At last count, there were over 35,000 Christian churches in the world. Any body of people which meets under a separate, autonomous authority which answers to no one higher, is a church. Therefore, every "Independent, Bible-Believing, KJV Only" assembly is a church with its own authority which answers to no one else. Before my conversion, I was a member of several Fundamentalist assemblies like this and there is the sense in these communities that "we alone are right in all we teach." The pastor is considered the final authority, which means that his interpretation of scripture in reference to doctrinal and moral teaching is the final word. Accept it and be welcome. Disagree and *"Please find the door, sir, and go find another body with whom you agree. There are many other assemblies from which to make your choice. We*

---

[83] John 17: 21

are right and they are wrong, but you please leave us and go take your chances with your soul. " Such an attitude is not the stuff of which family unity is made. For instance, there is not one Lutheran church, but three because ELCA, and LCMS, and the CLC are independent of each other. [84]

Using the analogy of the family, does a family unit have a single head with a single voice of authority, or can just anyone tell the family what to do and act as its head? Could I, as a man, just go to my neighbor's house and begin ordering around his wife and children? This is a ridiculous question, but I pose it to make a point. The Church is God's family on earth. As with all families and all covenant units, there is only one covenant head over it. Even using the Suzerainty treaties of which Calvinists are so fond, there is only one Suzerainty Great King. All other kingdoms are subservient to his rule, which means that what he and he alone says is the law of the kingdom.

If we put aside the familial model and view the Church using the Suzerainty model, there is one Suzerain, one Great King, Who is over all – our Lord Jesus Christ. He as King has left this kingdom and is bodily present in the eternal kingdom. Did He leave and put no one in charge in His absence? Were His last words before His Ascension *"Good luck figuring it out, guys!"*?

I have heard representatives from a number of different ecclesial bodies say *"We are the Church. All others are in error, and therefore cannot be the Church."* When I was in the PCA, I had a friend who used to wonder out loud how anyone outside of Presbyterian Calvinism could even be saved, even though he admitted, with great confusion, that they really showed signs of loving Jesus. His thinking was along the lines of *"The Church has the truth. Presbyterianism is the truth. All who love Jesus love the truth. Therefore, if they love Jesus, the*

---

[84] Liberal - Evangelical Lutheran Church in America (ELCA) ǀ Moderate - Lutheran Church / Missouri Synod (LCMS) ǀ Confessional, Church of the Lutheran Confession (CLC). Each body has its own headship, independent of the other, which means that despite calling themselves Lutheran, we have three different churches, not one.

Holy Spirit should bring them to be Presbyterians." I am sure that in their heart of hearts, some of his Anabaptist friends felt much the same way about him.

This is utter and complete chaos. This is not the unity which our Lord prayed for. This is not the unity of a family. I hope by now you, dear reader, have come to see God's intention to have a single family on earth, lead by a single covenant head. The Orthodox Church fits this paradigm. There is but one family led by one divine Head, Jesus Christ. All outside this communion and unity may, by virtue of their baptism, be in the covenant of God, but they are sitting outside the communion of the faithful and are not in the fullness of the faith.

At the end of his chapter on transcendence, and heading into the next chapter, which is on hierarchy, Bishop Sutton states: *"God is transcendent, and He establishes legal representatives who mediate life and death to earth."* [85]

Honestly, when I read sentences like this, I wonder if this gentleman even thinks about what he is writing. How does he belong to an ecclesial body which has no connection to the Early Church and the covenant authority established in the apostles? In his fifth principle of covenant, that of succession, Sutton says that covenant goes from generation to generation, yet he denies this to Orthodoxy by turning from the succession of bishops to establish his own little fiefdom.

Sutton goes on to state Samuel's warning: *"Rebellion is as the sin of witchcraft" (divination) – summarize the relationship between authority and idolatry. Rebellion is a rejection of some sort of representative authority of God, who by definition represents God."* [86]

Which is very serious business. An example of just how serious this is can be found in the first days of the Church. The representative authority of God,

---

[85] **THAT YOU MAY PROSPER** I Ray Sutton I Institute for Christian Economics I June 1987 I Page 40.

[86] Ibid I Page 42

152

Peter, is approached by two people who have joined themselves to the Church.

Acts 5:1 "But a certain man named Ananias, with Sapphira his wife, sold a possession, 2 And kept back part of the price, his wife also being privy to it, and brought a certain part, and laid it at the apostles' feet. 3 But Peter said, Ananias, why hath Satan filled thine heart to lie to the Holy Ghost, and to keep back part of the price of the land? 4Whiles it remained, was it not thine own? and after it was sold, was it not in thine own power? why hast thou conceived this thing in thine heart? _thou hast not lied unto men, but unto God._**"**

On page 43 of his book, Sutton speaks of visible authority. When I read this part of his book, still a Protestant but seeking and questioning, I realized that the claim of an of an "invisible Church made up of true believers" is an absolute farce! Without visible authority on the earth, God has no point from which to rule. It would be the same as a family without a father – chaos.

"Notice the progression from transcendence to hierarchy in this passage. Christ is raised and seated in heaven, and then His authority is planted on earth. The Lord declares Christ's transcendence, and then establishes Christ's visible sovereignty through the rule of His people as His authority." [87]

Okay, Bishop Sutton. Who? Who bears this visible rule over His people on earth from the very beginning? It was the apostles who were given authority over the Church to rule, with Peter being the first in honor. And in the principle of succession, it was only those who succeeded them who had the right to rule over the Church. No self-proclaimed bishop has any authority over anyone if he

---

[87] Ibid | Page 44

has not been ordained through the succession of authority handed down through the ages.

"There is no escape from the principle of man's God-given mediatory authority. If God's authorities do not rule, neither does He, in the sense of a public manifestation of authority. He manifests visible sovereignty through the visible authority of those who are invisible covenant to Him." [88]

The Church is also, according to Sutton, that same visible authority.

"The second section of the covenant presents Israel as the Lord's representative on the earth. They were a priesthood, a hierarchy...The Church in New Testament times serves a similar function. The New Testament compares the Church's liturgy to the Old Testament's: "... golden bowls full of incense, which are the prayers of the saints" (Rev. 5:8; cf. 8:3)" [89]

This principle of visible authority creates massive problems for the Calvinist faith.

25.2 The visible church, which is also catholic or universal under the gospel (not confined to one nation, as before under the law), consists of all those throughout the world *that profess the true religion*; and of their children: and is the kingdom of the Lord Jesus Christ, the house and family of God, *out of which there is no ordinary possibility of salvation.* [90]

---

[88] Ibid | Page 45

[89] Ibid | Page 46

[90] Westminster Confession of Faith | Section 25 | Of the Church

154

The visible Church (i.e. the one with Christ's authority) has the true religion. Okay, which one is the true religion? Anabaptists? Seventh Day Adventists? Presbyterians? Episcopalians? Do you see the problem here? Each one of these, as well as numerous other bodies I did not mention, would loudly claim that they have the true Christian religion. You have never seen some of the arguments I have seen on the Internet between competing Protestant apologists. The anathemas and maledictions between them can fly hot and heavy over a single point of doctrine such as infant baptism!

It gets even worse.

25.5 *The purest churches under heaven are subject both to mixture and error; and some have so degenerated, as to become no churches of Christ, but synagogues of Satan. Nevertheless, there shall be always a church on earth, to worship God according to his will.* [91]

Okay, Calvinists, how do you tell when a congregation has become a synagogue of Satan? Didn't our Lord promise that His Church would never do that? There was no idea in fifteen hundred years of Church history that the Church would teach error. When error presented itself to the Church, councils were called and the issue was settled. All errors may have had their origination within the Church, but with the convoking of a council, heretics such as Arias and Marcion were exposed and their teachings condemned.

This quote from the Westminster Confession is a horror, for the Bible says that the Church is the pillar and ground of truth. [92] The idea that the Church,

---

[91] Ibid

[92] 1 Timothy 3:15

as the pillar and ground of truth, would tolerate or teach heresy opened the door for the ecclesial and theological chaos we see today. This is why I have come to reject the Roman Catholic Church as the Church. They have left the faith which the Early Fathers taught and have invented things not known by the earliest Christians. If they were the Church, they could not teach error.

The Church is the congregation of God. It is God's people gathered together under a representative authority (king) and a covenant authority (Christ the Great High Priest). It is the kingdom of God on earth, representing the kingdom to the unbelievers around them. This congregation was organized in the OT with Moses in the wilderness as the proper worship and ordinances were established and a place of worship, the tabernacle, was established. When the covenant authority, the high priest, Caiaphas, ordered Jesus put to death, the covenant was destroyed between Israel and God and a New Covenant was established. But the kingdom merely changed hands. In Matthew 21: 33-46, we see Jesus prophesying this change of administration. National Israel, represented as the husbandmen in the parable, are destroyed and the kingdom is given to the Israel of God, which is the Church. [93]

As national Israel was God's visible representative authority to the world, so the Orthodox Church is today. Rome has left the unity of the Church and Protestant bodies are man-made from pride and rebellion.

Ethics: As I discuss the ethics of covenant relationships, it is helpful to remember that I came out of the same Presbyterian understanding of covenant which I am criticizing in this book. Thus, when I first wrote this book, I understood ethics along the lines of the establishment of certain laws by which the covenant is maintained. As I have grown in my faith and come to see the covenant now as relationship rather than legal covenant, I have changed my view

---

[93] Matthew 21:43 Therefore say I unto you, The kingdom of God shall be taken from you, and given to a nation bringing forth the fruits thereof.

of it. I find it uncomfortable to think of a relationship of love being based on the establishment and keeping of a bunch of laws. This was the mindset of the Pharisees, yet for all their religious duties, which Christ acknowledged, He had this to say to them:

Matthew 23:23 Woe unto you, scribes and Pharisees, hypocrites! for ye pay tithe of mint and anise and cummin, and have omitted the weightier matters of the law, judgment, mercy, and faith: these ought ye to have done, and not to leave the other undone.

The Pharisees were very good at keeping rules. They stank at charity, which is the heart of the Gospel. Instead of representing God's love to a world in need of seeing it, they beat orphans and widows out of a shekel and turned from their duties to their parents to make a show of giving money to the Temple. Establishing laws and fastidiously keeping them may work well for treaties between Suzerain kings. It is not at all a good basis for a relationship of love.

What is the difference between a father and a judge? What is the difference in how a man would react to an offense by his wife, whom he loves intensely, and the same offense being done by a women he doesn't even know? If you can see the potential difference in response in these different relationships, then you can begin to get a grasp on the problem I have with the strictly juridical view of God as Judge. This view seems to be the overwhelming view of God in the Western Church, for while God is spoken of as Father, and His love is spoken of in terms of extreme compassion for mankind, the description of His actions in judgment those who have failed seem inconsistent with the extreme love of a father for a child. Bluntly put, there are times I heard the judgment of God described in terms more akin to the actions of a tyrant waiting to pounce upon an erring rebel than the actions of a father seeking at all costs to restore a wayward child.

This extreme description of God's judicial actions, and His anger in general against the whole human race, is nowhere more pronounced than in Calvinism. Even the forgiveness offered to sinners who are fortunate to be among the elect is not that of the father of the Prodigal forgetting his dignity to run out and greet his wayward son. As I have noted earlier, beginning with Adam, Calvinists view our relationship to God as that of a vassal slave to his master rather than the longing of the Prodigal's father. And the descriptions of God's absolute hatred towards the rest of the human race – the non elect – are enough to make you think He is a perpetually angry deity whose wrath is only barely held back by the pleadings of Jesus.

As an Orthodox Christian, one of the problematic things I see with Western theology, one that may well have led to the Reformation, is the influence of Roman fascination with law and law-keeping as Christianity established itself in Roman society. I see this as the difference between a relationship of love and a state of servitude. In the former, love changes being, so I become more and more like my beloved in my thoughts, desires, and deeds. My deeds come from a true desire to bless my beloved and make him/her happy. In the latter, law makes me obey out of fear of punishment or loss. While outwardly obedient to the laws imposed upon me, I may be absolutely seething within against those who are over me, and I remain unchanged internally. There is neither union with nor concern for the one who holds rule over me.

As I see it, the Western Church seems to be terribly rule oriented. One of the problematic issues of the Medieval time in which the Reformation took place was the issue of merit. As Rev. Ralph Smith shows in his book on the eternal covenant, the Reformers made a distinct swerve away from any hint that man could in any way merit anything from God. The idea of man obeying a specific set of laws in order to either obtain enough merit to be salvific, or to get one an early out from Purgatory, became a real problem. When I see how finely some of the actions of man are divided into "sin/not sin" in the Western Church,

158

I fail to see a covenant relationship which is built on the unitive principle of love. Salvation becomes not an act of loving union with Christ, but rather a ledger in which good deeds (i.e. law-keeping for merit) are racked up. This is what drove Luther, who was training to be a lawyer, out of his mind, and eventually led to the Reformation.

It appears to me that the Roman idea of merit and law keeping, and the soteriology that developed from this, came to a point that it was putrid in the nostrils of the Reformers. But in turning away from the Roman concept of merit, they swerved entirely off course in the other direction, creating a beast called the covenant of grace in which God supposedly does everything in the covenant for us because they see the law as having to be kept perfectly, even to the very tiniest jot and tittle. Thus, if a man cannot do this, he cannot be saved.

Such a steep demand for legal perfection rather than relational grace in love, means that since man cannot keep the law perfectly, someone must do it for him. Thus came the idea of a covenant of grace in which Christ does all the work of covenant keeping with the Father on our behalf. This in turn, leads to the false idea of imputed righteousness, the covering of a man's soul by the Christ's righteousness which is both perfect and legally necessary to obtain salvation. The huge emphasis on man's doing works to obtain salvation made the Reformers leery of anything which smacked of our efforts in having a relationship with God. They saw any appeal to man's cooperation with God as Pelegianism.

The Calvinist view cannot be a covenant, for in a covenant relationship, as analogized by marriage in the Bible, both sides make vows of love and fidelity and then live up to them throughout the course of the marriage. And no one can do this for another in a marriage as a substitute or representative. The great separation in the West began because Luther saw God as the Great Judge whose law he could not keep, even in the tiniest bit. He did not see God as Spouse and his actions as the response of love, but only that of fear of punishment for not keeping the law perfectly.

It is interesting to note that the emphasis of Orthodox soteriology, anthropology, and theology has to do with ontological realities which appear to me to be at best muted in the Western Church. The Orthodox Church places strong emphasis on our being (ousia) and how what we are becoming in Christ unites us to Him. How then does the covenant principle of ethics tie in with this? The Orthodox Church sees the purpose of salvation as the healing of a sick soul, not the perfect keeping of a set of laws. This is why the Early Fathers of the Church described the Eucharist as "the medicine of immortality." This is not to say that we have no such thing as God's law in the Orthodox Church, but rather, the emphasis is on theosis, the union between Christ and the soul which creates a change in the person.

Salvation in Orthodoxy is seen as ontological change into Christlikeness, created by this union of love between Christ and the soul. The more I become like Christ in my very being (ousia) the deeper the reality of salvation becomes for me. It is a therapeutic and healing process which changes one's intrinsic being. Ultimately, as I am changed into the likeness of God by sharing in the divine nature, I find the very completeness and purpose for which I was created. Man is a communal being because the Trinity is a community of love. This does not appear to be the major thrust of Western soteriological understanding. I am not saying that this theory is not present in the West, but it is muted in comparison to the great emphasis on keeping of the law.

The great heresies of the Early Church had to do with the anthropological definitions of Christ as man. These definitions are important because the ousia (being) of man was that very thing which was corrupted by the fall. Once corrupted, man's nature was unable to enter into the unitive depth of the divine covenant relationship for which it was designed. Adam's goal and purpose was to enter deeper and deeper into the unitive reality of theosis – becoming like God – by the exercise of faith. The law of the Covenant of Works, which Calvinists see Adam breaking, was not a law at all. What Adam was given was an exercise of faith in love, a chance to trust God and thus deepen the relationship of love through that act of trust. The fullness, the completeness of Adam's being was to be found in submissive, self-donative union to God. The fruit of the tree appeared to offer Adam a way to that fullness of being (knowledge of good and evil). As the saying goes, "Actions speak louder than words," and Adam's actions said in effect *"You are not my fullness, God. I don't trust in you to be my fullness. I believe this fruit will bring me to completeness."* Adam sought his true ousia (being) outside of communion with God. But only communion with God, with He Who is true Being, makes us truly and fully what we are intended to be.

At the same time, I cannot deny that in the East as well as the West, we do make vows upon our baptism in to the congregation of God. We do promise to do certain acts and eschew other acts. These vows are at the heart of covenant, as we see in many places in scripture where oaths/sanctions are set forth as part of entering the covenant relationship. Because these oaths are taken, there must be a set of ethics (behaviors) upon which these vows are based and to which one must pledge fidelity. What exactly are these ethics and how do I keep them?

I do not seeing ethics in the purely Roman legal sense as a set of rules to be kept to the finest degree, but rather as the understanding of what the actions are that will please the one I love and what the actions are that will hurt the one I love. They are principles of behavior towards my beloved. When I make my vows, I am saying in essence, *"I will do nothing which will hurt you, make you sorrowful, or put a barrier between our union of love."*

Ethics as law in a Suzerainty treaty is fine to define limits of acceptable actions and responses towards the one who is the Great King. Approaching a marriage in such a way seems like the kiss of death to me. A set of rules can be kept without necessarily having a relationship of utter commitment to one another. There is no sense in the treaty/contract of two kings that they are entering into a deeply felt committed relationship with each other. Both sides see the benefit of the contract and both sides enter into it. One does so to increase his glory and kingdom, the other does so for protection, both from the greater king and others. In fact, as I think of it further, it seems that the more laws which are stipulated in the treaty, the less trust there is between the parties.

When I think of the relationship of husband and wife, their union of love, and the life lived between them of seeking an ever closer union, I have a hard time reducing the ethics of our covenant relationship with our divine Bridegroom to a series of laws which we must keep perfectly or lose our salvation. Ethics has been called "the law-keeping aspect of the covenant" but I really hate to see this put in such terms. Where would you find a marriage in which the spouses refer to each other through a system of laws they have set up to rule their household? What kind of intimate and loving relationship is that? Therefore, I find the Reformed approach to be problematic at best. Relationships are defined and kept by actions which are self-sacrificial and self-donative, and because of that supercede the establishment of behavior regulated by rules.

According to Jesus, the only act which breaks the marital covenant is to physically unite with one with whom you have not made the covenant of marriage. An act of covenant self-giving to another, adultery, is a real act of breaking covenant unity with one's spouse.

Mat 5:32 But I say unto you, That whosoever shall put away his wife, saving for the cause of fornication, causeth her to commit adultery: and whosoever shall marry her that is divorced committeth adultery.

All other acts, such as being a grouchy person, may strain the marriage and its relationship, but they do not break that physical sign/bond which occurred in the nuptial bed. This is why our Lord said that except for the act of adultery, any one who divorces his wife and marries another commits adultery himself. He mentioned no other basis for divorce, which is both the act and the visible sign of a broken relationship. In essence Jesus gave only one ethic to the covenant of marriage which if kept, continued the marriage, and if broken, ended it. The nuptial act is the consummation of covenant making. Without it, there is no covenant, with it, the union is made totally complete. Therefore, to perform this act with another is to make a covenant with that person – and thus destroy the covenant vow of fidelity in love which you made with the one you married. How does this act of total self-donation relate to our covenant marriage with our divine Bridegroom? What does it mean for the principle of covenant ethics and the vows we make based on those ethics?

I see it as meaning that the single ethic of the covenant is love.

If that is the simple and only ethic of the New Covenant, then it is easy. If the ethic of the New Covenant is love, then following the analogy of earthly marriage, the only thing that can break that covenant relationship is if I commit spiritual adultery by giving myself to someone else other than my divine Bridegroom. Then the question becomes rather *"By what action do I commit adultery and completely give myself to something else other than Christ?"*

In the Old Covenant, God had to tell the Israelites what these commandments were because they did not have the Holy Spirit dwelling within. Their rudimentary understanding of God did not understand that you cannot claim to love God and yet bow down to pagan idols and give them your love. They did not understand that if you violate God's natural law by living a life sexual immorality, you are saying to God *"I don't love you. Go away and leave me alone because I love this action more than I love you."* Any action chosen more than being with Jesus is adultery. Don't tell me how much you love God if you are on the golf course every Sunday morning. Do you get the picture?

In the New Covenant, love is one ethic stressed. From ten commandments, and six hundred and thirteen laws, Jesus broke down the ethics of our covenant relationship with God into two simple statements: love God supremely, and love your neighbor in the same way you love yourself. St.

Francis said *"Love God and do what you will."* How could he say that? Because love is always concerned with the good of the other, even to the denial of the self. Love is the single law and apex of covenant ethics. Jesus made this clear when He boiled down all the laws of Judaism to two ethics: love God supremely and your neighbor as yourself.

Seems to me all the rest is window dressing.

Oaths/Sanctions: Even though the ethics of the New Covenant has been boiled down by Christ to just two commands – loving God supremely and loving others supremely – there is still the reality of making promises to perform acts of love to God and our fellow man as we enter into the Church. To take an oath means that I am accountable for my actions, and a self-maledictory oath means I am calling down upon myself, in the presence of witnesses, certain penalties which come with breaking those vows. This is the legal sense, from which Sutton bases all his suppositions.

But familial love does not work this way. Familial love is not based on meeting a constant checklist of legal decrees, but is rather the expression of union which results from the actions of the two who are involved. It is better seen as *cause and effect* rather than checking off a list.

As an example: I can stop at the florists and buy flowers because it is Mother's Day and I am expected to do so. This is the law, this is the unwritten expectation for all husbands/fathers on that day. It is legally precise, I can check the box that I have done that which is expected, but kind of relationship do I have with my wife if I do this because it is expected rather than wanting to in order to bring joy to my wife?

A desire to bless and make happy my wife will motivate me to pick up flowers on an average Wednesday night and bring them home. By living with and coming to know my wife, I have come to know that she just loves blue snapdragons, so I get her a big bouquet of them at the local supermarket. This is not law. This is relationship working itself out in a practical way. By taking such action (cause) the relationship deepens and grows (effect). I love my wife and I take pleasure in seeing the happiness in her eyes when she receives the flowers.

In this familial example, suppose I never take the time to bring flowers, take out to dinner, or give compliments on good housekeeping. Is there a law that says I have to do these things? Not really. But will there be a cause and effect relationship in my failure to do them? Of course. The relationship will never deepen and I will never experience the joy of a unitive love so deep that my wife and I almost breathe with the same breath. In this understanding of marriage and the oaths taken in the wedding ceremony, the self-maledictory part of my promise to "love, cherish, and protect" is that my wife's heart is slowly turned from me. The curse which comes upon me is not that of a certain set of prescribed punishments, but rather of losing something that could be a great blessing to me – loving and ever deepening union with my wife.

We can do the same thing with the One who is our divine Bridegroom. Roman law looks at sinners as receiving punishments and even the tortures of hell as the penalty for willing sin. In Orthodoxy, there is no such place as hell. There is something far worse – a broken relationship in which being in the very presence of Christ is torment to the sinner who does not want Christ.

This was one of the intriguing things I found when investigating Orthodoxy. The same fire of Christ's passionate love blesses those who love Christ, but torments those who want nothing to do with Him. I found this to be much more just than the idea that if I ate one bite too much of the best ice cream in the world, Hagen-Daz Coffee, God would unleash all His ire on me as a wretched sinner. This kind of niggling law-keeping was driving me crazy trying to figure out how to escape punishment. No, it is not that at all. It is what I become in this life which determines how I will experience the next life. It is about relationship.

The true penalty is the loss of relationship. Outside of Christ, there is no life, no joy, no union of love, and no reality of true personhood. As sentient beings, we are made for communion, both with others and with God. The lack of this communion for eternity is the self-imposed penalty we place on ourselves for driving away the One who loves us. As fire and water cannot combine, neither can the selfless love of Christ be poured into a vessel that will not give back. The whole basis of love is a complete self-emptying and receiving. In making covenant with Christ as our Spouse, the oath is simply to love. The self-imposed sanction is to deprive ourselves of love forever.

In the family understanding of the Church, the self-maledictory penalty is a cause and effect penalty. The cause is our willing separation from union with Christ. The effect is that we lose the inheritance, which is blessing, and instead inherit curse.

The principle of oaths/sanctions cuts across the teaching that once one is saved, that salvation cannot be lost. It destroys the false Calvinist doctrine of the Perseverance of the Saints. As I explained earlier, this idea comes from both a misunderstanding of the term "saved" and believing in the idea of a legal (forensic) state of justification between ourselves and God which cannot be annulled. Such thinking violates covenant principles and cannot be correct.

Bishop Sutton uses the standard Protestant line to avoid the reality that people can break off a relationship.

"Apostasy is real. People can fall away. Question: Fall away from what? They fall from the visible covenant. If they never come back and repent, then they were never truly converted to begin with." [94]

"Should he fall away from the faith, his assurance is lost. The easiest

---

[94] **THAT YOU MAY PROSPER** I Ray Sutton I Institute for Christian Economics I June 1987 I Page 81.

166

way to understand the apostate's position is to compare it to a judge's granting of a suspended sentence with probation. He does not declare them "Not Guilty." He gives them a suspended sentence with probation to see what they can do with their freedom. He reserves the right to put them back into prison at any time." [95]

I hope by now you recognize Sutton's egregious error. He calls upon the standard line of Calvinist reasoning in regards to mankind, even as those who have been saved. In Calvinism, mankind is not sons and daughters. We are rebellious vassals under a legal status of probation. God is not loving Father striving to bring the Prodigal (apostate) back to the household. God is Judge, and a fierce and terrifying one. Just ask Luther. The vision of his own legal imperfection before the Great Judge drove him to despair. Even after hours in the confessional, Luther's tormented mind could find no peace. Only when he came up with the non-covenantal position of faith alone, and the legal justification he imagined went with it, did he find a kind of peace for his tormented mind.

Listen to the linguistic gymnastics in which Sutton engages to avoid admitting that men can be faithful to their oaths for decades and then fall away:

"Every covenant with the exception of Christ's on the cross was unconditional.

(First mistake: You have stated in your book that oaths/sanctions are at the heart of covenant. Oaths and sanctions are the conditions by which we either keep or break our covenant relationship. Since this is so, then there can be no such thing as an unconditional covenant. What you have just said would mean that the covenant Moses entered into was

---

[95] Ibid | Page 82

unconditional. If so, then why did God nearly kill him for failing to fulfill the conditions of the covenant?)

Even the first covenant with Adam was unconditional. Adam had done nothing to be created or to earn the garden.

(Well, if you look at it Adam as a vassal slave, then yes, I can see that. Vassals have to enter into agreements. But there were no conditions because Adam was the son of God, and as I said, sons do not have to make agreements to be in the family and part of that covenant.)

The terms of not eating the tree of the knowledge of good and evil were in the context of the unconditionality of creation.

(How could this be? What in the world does Sutton mean by the unconditionality of creation? The terms of not eating the tree were the ethics of remaining in covenant relationship with his Father).

We can call them the terms of unconditionality. The only person who entered a purely conditional covenant was Christ. But once He met its terms and died on the Cross, it became unconditional to everyone who received it.

This completely contradicts everything that Sutton has said in his covenant principles of ethics and oaths/sanctions. From Genesis right up to Christ, the actions of God toward His people are based on covenant faithfulness or covenant disobedience, with the accompanying blessings and curses.

God the Father will never revoke His declaration that Christ perfectly

168

met the terms of the covenant. The unconditionality of the covenant is assured eternally. As long as one lives in Christ, he is under an unconditional covenant.

(Half right: Christ met the terms of which covenant? The corporate covenant in which He represented all mankind and by His perfect keeping of the terms of that covenant, restored all mankind to God. That corporate covenant, first represented by the Yom Kippur corporate sacrifice, is vastly different than the individual covenant which each person has to make with Christ.

Your statement in which you state "as long as one lives in Christ he is in an unconditional covenant" is *egregiously* wrong. Even Christ, as the Last Adam, is in covenant, which means that it is conditional. The same conditions of ethics and oaths/sanctions applied to Him as man. If they did not, it was not a covenant, according to your own definitions and principles, sir! Furthermore, He could not be man the same as us if the covenant did not apply in the same manner as it did to Adam, that is, blessing for obedience and curse for disobedience.

And don't you see that by saying this, you admit that all mankind is under conditional covenant, for if a man falls away from Christ, he has broken his covenant relationship, which means that it is conditional, not unconditional!

The reason the corporate covenant will never fail is because the Blood of Christ is eternally offered as the YOM KIPPUR [96] sacrifice of the

---

[96] **Hebrews 9:11 But Christ being come an high priest of good things to come, by a greater and more perfect tabernacle, not made with hands, that is to say, not of this building;**

corporate covenant on the altar of heaven. And Christ, the Living Word, will never turn away from the Father. The covenant is therefore eternal, and in that sense, you could say it is now unconditional, being permanently fulfilled. All covenant relationships have conditions. Even you admit this when you say that Christ "met the terms of the covenant." But don't try to make this a case for Perseverance of the Saints, since we can and do turn from Christ as covenant breakers!

This does not mean people in the covenant cannot apostatize. We enter an unconditional covenant, but there are terms of unconditionality." [97]

(Wait a minute! Make up your mind! Terms belong to conditionality! You are not even keeping your own principles!)

One more quote from Bishop Sutton should show us just how far afield this man has gone in his attempt to salvage the indefensible:

"The covenant can be terminated, or dissolved. The continuity of all the covenants– God to God, God to man, and man to man – is in fact dissoluble." [98]

Did we not just read the following statement: **"Every covenant with the exception of Christ's on the cross was unconditional,"** meaning that it cannot be broken, terminated, or *dissolved*? I am shocked that a brilliant and theologically astute man such as Sutton is willing to fall on his intellectual sword

---

[97] THAT YOU MAY PROSPER | Ray Sutton | Institute for Christian Economics | June 1987 | Page 81.

[98]— Ibid Page 111

by writing such self-contradictory nonsense in a vain attempt to defend the Calvinist position. Forgive me if my speech here appears to lack charity, but I find this kind of double-talk more than a little annoying.

Calvinist covenant understanding is based upon a foundation of numerous errors and erroneous doctrines. Adam as vassal slave rather than son, believing in a term called total depravity (which is not found in the Bible), insisting that Christ does all our covenant oath keeping for us rather than us having any responsibility to our baptismal vows, and finally creating a class of men called the elect who can never lose the inheritance of eternal life because they are declared legally not guilty in the heavenly court of law. It is just one error after another, the worst being that they conflate the corporate and the individual covenant, making the establishment of the New Covenant between Christ and the Father to be the same thing as our individual covenant with Christ as Bride and Bridegroom.

In regards to oath/sanctions in the scriptures, there are two covenants which are mentioned in the Bible, a corporate covenant and a personal covenant. Both of these have oaths/sanctions. The corporate covenant is found in Leviticus 16. It is the Yom Kippur sacrifice which renews the corporate covenant between God and mankind (being represented by His people, Israel). In the corporate covenant, the high priest acts as the covenant head and makes sacrifice for mankind, represented by national Israel. All oaths are of this covenant are fulfilled perfectly in Christ. In Hebrews 7-10, we see Christ acting as the Great High Priest in the "tabernacle not made with hands." In doing so, as the Last Adam (Aw-dham means mankind), all mankind renews and eternally keeps the covenant with the Father. Adam is restored. Mankind as family is healed because Christ assumes human nature and heals it, returning it to union with the Father.

The redemption of all creation and mankind as family opens the possibility of a personal covenant through which individuals may enter the covenant congregation and partake of the salvation offered. This covenant, like the corporate covenant, has oaths/sanctions to it. The difference is that in the corporate covenant, the One Who is Covenant Head has kept all the oaths/sanctions perfectly, so that mankind is once again in relationship with God. The state of Edenic innocence is restored and added to, for now not only is mankind innocent before God, but mankind is also, in Christ, in right standing with the Father.

The individual covenant, which we see being made in order to enter the congregation, is shown not in Yom Kippur, but in circumcision. That act of covenant cutting made one a member of the congregation. In the New Covenant, the congregation, or Church, is called the Body of Christ. I hope you see the unity there and how when we cut covenant with Christ as our divine Bridegroom, we are entered into His congregation and unite with His Body. Being in His Body gives us not a legal declaration of perfect righteousness, but a individual reality of righteousness which God sees.

What are the oaths we make upon entering the Church? They are all the same thing, promises to love Christ/God supremely and before any other created thing, either people or creature. Take any commandment which man can break and put it in the context of loving God alone:

Thou shalt not steal – I love God more than things, therefore, things are of little consequence to me. My love for God means that I do not lust after things. My love for God also means that I do not wish to hurt Him by doing that which He has said is wrong. Because I love, I obey.

Thou shalt not commit adultery – Because I love God more than the pleasuring of my body, I will be chaste to show my love for Him. I will do so because this is what He said He wants, and because I love Him, I want to do the things He wants. The same goes with any other form of recreational pleasuring, such as smoking marijuana. I love God, therefore I will seek to find in Him alone that joy and pleasure that drugs can only as a false substitute for Him.

172

SUMMARY

The Judgment is not about how perfectly we have kept a bunch of rules, right down to the minutia of one more bite of Hagen-Daz going from enjoyment to gluttony. Jesus addressed this with the Pharisees when he told them that they strained out gnats to meet the requirements of the Law, but forgot about the greater issue of love and mercy.

Our judgment will be whether we have loved Him supremely above all other things in life. If we have loved Him, then like a spouse united to her husband, we will find His presence will be a delight and joy. If we have loved others and hated Him, the curse we will have brought upon ourselves will be to be eternally in the presence of One whose reality is a torment because He is so different from what we are.

THE FAMILY CONTINUES FOREVER

I want to dedicate a single chapter to Sutton's fifth covenant principle, succession, because it answers a very important question which is tied in with the principles of both transcendence and hierarchy: which ecclesiastical body is the Church? There are as many definitions of what constitutes the Church as there are ecclesial assemblies. Not all of them can be correct. In fact, there can only be one correct answer. I want to use this fifth principle to establish where you may find the Church which was established on earth by God.

To begin with, we need to properly understand what is meant by the word church. Let's start with the definitions found in the scriptures.

Ekklesia is the NT Greek word which is translated into our English word church. An examination of the Greek word "ekklesia" reveals that the word is properly translated into English as "assembly" or "congregation." It is used to refer to a group of persons that are organized together for a common purpose and who meet together.

There is another word in the scriptures which has the exact same meaning. It is the Hebrew word "qāhēl," found, of course, in the OT. It is interesting to see this connection when reading Hebrews 2:12.

Hebrews 2:12 Saying, I will declare thy name unto my brethren, in the midst of the church will I sing praise unto thee.

This is a direct quote of Psalms 22:22. So we see that when the writer of Hebrews sees the word "qāhēl" in the OT, he has no trouble identifying it as meaning church. The church is a congregation or assembly of people gathered together for a distinct purpose. That purpose is worship.

The structure of the first congregation was a covenant structure. Within it was covenant representative authority, the high priest, and later on, the representative authority of the king of Israel. The latter was not the original intention, for God identified Himself as the authority over Israel. It was the hardness of the Israelite hearts that demanded a king similar to those of the neighboring pagan tribes had. They did not want God as king, but would have a man rule over them. Hundreds of years and many human kings later, the true King would incarnate Himself and offer Himself to the people. They rejected Him, and in doing so, rejected the authority of God over them. The final nail was driven into the coffin of the Old Covenant when the covenant representative ordered the death of Christ. Acting for the people as their representative, in Caiaphas the high priest, the congregation rejected their King and their covenant with God and doomed themselves to receive the full measure of the covenant curse, which fell in full upon them in AD 70.

The first representative was Adam. Created as son into the covenant of the Trinity, Adam was both priest (covenant representative) and prince (authority representative) to Creation.

In Sutton's second principle, we see this rule: *"Second, the covenant taught a concept of authority, or hierarchy, based on representation."* [99]

We see the exact same thing in the man, Jesus, who is both covenant representative (Great High Priest) and authority representative (King of Creation) of the Father.

The fall severed covenant authority from mankind. Adam performed an act of covenant obeisance to the evil one, and in doing so, made a covenant with him. Although it was a false covenant, it had the same structure, although in reverse. The blessing of this false covenant is not life, but death. In fact, every blessing of God which comes from a covenant union with Him, is reversed in the false covenant with the evil one. Think of any blessing, any good which men seek, and reverse it and you have the false blessing of the covenant with death. Peace becomes war. Love becomes selfishness. Giving becomes taking. Blessing others becomes using others. The inheritance of life becomes an inheritance of death. To bind one's self to the evil one by an act of covenant obedience means an end which is annihilation of all that makes us human.

This act of covenant obeisance also stripped from Adam the position of authority representative. Authority (power) was now usurped by the wicked one. A false representative authority pictures god not as loving father, but as stern and implacable deity. This demanding god puts into man's imagination false demands of authority, with correspondent threats of curse if not followed. These false demands are most highlighted by the reprehensible human sacrifices which are offered upon the altars of the false pagan gods. Innocent children are burned alive to insure that a curse of bad harvest does not fall upon them. This also an attack on the true covenant itself, for the principle of succession, which comes through the firstborn male, is attacked as children are offered in appeasement to a false god of a false covenant.

---

[99] **THAT YOU MAY PROSPER** I **Ray Sutton** I **Institute for Christian Economics** I **June 1987** I **Page 6.**

This false covenant cannot terminate the true covenant of the Trinity. What it has done is to steal the representational authority from the son of God (Adam) and place it in the hands of a thief. We see the thief almost bragging of this theft as he tempts the Christ:

Luk 4:6 And the devil said unto him, All this power will I give thee, and the glory of them: for that is delivered unto me; and to whomsoever I will I give it. 7 If thou therefore wilt worship me, all shall be thine.

It is noteworthy that Christ does not dispute this claim of ownership of the power (authority) over Creation. Also noteworthy is the threefold attempt of the wicked one to get Christ to make an act of covenant fidelity to him, which utterly fails. It is the beginning of the end of the usurpation of authority.

The temptation in the Garden was to have autonomous and complete authority, not representational authority, which is dependant upon the One Who is the Greater. Adam's true personhood was to be found in communion with God, a communion of utter self-abandonment, a complete dependency upon God. Our authority as priests and kings in the eschaton world after the General Resurrection will come from our union with our Father, not separate from Him. All that we have, and the fullness of being human, will be found in our participation and union in the eternal covenant relationship. When Adam turned from this dependency on the command (Word) of God, expecting to find completion as a person in the knowledge of good and evil, he instead found himself stripped of all that made him a true person. That which he expected to fulfill his life plunged him into a state of separation which is called death.

What this did not do, however, was to end the familial relationship of God to mankind and to Creation. Therefore, God continued to deal with mankind in covenant. There was no one else who could represent God to Creation, so Adam continued to do so, but in a covenant relationship that was now damaged and could not fulfill the promised blessings it had originally offered in Eden.

Through the generations, God established representatives for His covenant and authority over Creation. We see a clue of this in Genesis 14: 18 with the blessing of Abram by Melchizedek, who is identified as both king and priest. God is not without a covenant representative, even though that representation has been corrupted by sin.

Almost immediately after this covenant blessing is given by Melchizedek, we see God begin to deal with Abram with the intention of establishing His covenant family once again on earth as a nation of priests and kings (remember, this was the original intent in the Garden). Abraham receives the promise of a family, which will be the congregation of the Lord:

Gen 15:5 And he brought him forth abroad, and said, Look now toward heaven, and tell the stars, if thou be able to number them: and he said unto him, So shall thy seed be.

So shall thy seed be, that is, all those who will be the congregation of the Lord. How do I know this?

Gal 3:29 And if ye be Christ's, ***then are ye Abraham's seed,*** **and heirs according to the promise.**

All those who are in Christ, that is, all believers of all time, both those who looked forward to his coming, and those who have entered into Him by baptism, are the seed of Abraham, and the congregation of the Lord. We are the congregation of the Lord, the innumerable gathering of the saints throughout the ages, who will be the covenant family forever; who as sons and daughters of God will rule and reign the cosmos with Him, in subjection to Him as the Great Suzerain, but nonetheless called kings and queens in the Church eternal.

178

In order to have a people and a witness among mankind, God now chooses one man as His representative authority and establishes a congregation of people who are covenanted to Him. It is under the authority of Moses, this congregation is organized as a worship body. A tabernacle is constructed in the wilderness. This is a place where the covenant offerings can be made for the sins of the people by the various offerings of the Levitical priesthood, and for the sin of the nation by the offering of Yom Kippur.

In the book of Hebrews we see something important about this worship.

Hbr 8:4 For if he were on earth, he should not be a priest, seeing that there are priests that offer gifts according to the law: 5 Who serve unto the example and shadow of heavenly things, as Moses was admonished of God when he was about to make the tabernacle: for, See, saith he, that thou make all things according to the pattern shewed to thee in the mount.

The worship now established on earth is a witness to all Creation of the reality of the heavenly. So important is this worship that Moses is admonished (a very *strong* warning) not to trifle with it. There is a pattern to be followed, and God was not interested in man's ideas to make the worship better.

Christ came to national Israel, the covenant people, to offer Himself as their divine Spouse, their King, and the possessor of the inheritance. Their response was to kill him. [100] When they did, several things happened.

This act ended the covenant with national Israel as spouse to God. When you kill the one with whom you are in covenant, there is no more covenant. A wife who kills her husband ends that covenant between them. This is what Israel did when they murdered their divine Spouse. The symbol of this termination of the covenant was the rending of the veil from top to bottom (heaven to earth).

---

[100] Matthew 21: 38-39

The veil covered the Holiest of All where Yom Kippur was offered once a year to renew the covenant between God and Israel. The Holiest of All was exposed to the world. Being thus exposed, it was defiled and rendered ceremonially unfit to ever be used again. The end of the Old Covenant had now begun. Full termination would take place in a few years with the destruction of Jerusalem in AD 70. The New Covenant in Christ's Blood was inaugurated.

The representative authority was stripped from national Israel. We see this in the Parable of the Wicked Husbandmen. The husbandmen, who are in charge of the vineyard and therefore bear the authority to act on behalf of the owner as his visible representative, are taken out and given retributive justice for their evil deed. The fact that they are shown to be killed in the parable points to the fact that the covenant can never be renewed with them again because they are dead to it. Those who believe that national Israel has a future as the covenant representative of God have no basis for this belief, based on the parable.

This act did not, however, end the eternal covenant and God's intention that it continue as a means of blessing to all Creation. Because of this intention, just as when He submerged the world in judgment for its wickedness yet found Moses to carry the covenant forward, so now Christ is raised to new life and a New Covenant. The link between Christ and the congregation of God's people, which has been left widowed by the act of the high priest, is so close that the Church is now called The Body of Christ.

A covenant continues from generation to generation. This is Sutton's final principle, succession, one that we see repeated in scripture numerous times, and yet another one that he also ignores. It appears from scripture that there are through the centuries different covenant heads, first-born men who are an Adam to the covenant, but while they lead God's people, they cannot make the blood redemption necessary to redeem the covenant and re-establish it permanently upon a permanent sacrifice. There is no replacement or fulfillment of the covenant, only changes of visible authority.

180

When the Last Adam arrives, something happens which shows us a change of covenant:

"A meal is often associated with worship. Why? It is a way of confirming a covenant that has previously been cut. In the suzerain covenants, the soon-to-die suzerain would gather all of his followers together at a special ceremony involving a sacred meal. He would require them to pledge an oath of allegiance to his successor. Then, after he died, the successor would have another ceremony and meal. The followers would again pledge an oath and renew their covenant to seal legally and ritually the transfer of power." [101]

It is certainly significant that our Lord takes the occasion of the Passover, a meal of covenant establishment, and at that meal, declares the New Covenant in His Blood. This is the meal of the soon-to-die suzerain. What is the second meal, the one which followed the death and established the new order?

Luke 22:15 And he said unto them, With desire I have desired to eat this Passover with you before I suffer: 16 For I say unto you, I will not any more eat thereof, until it be fulfilled in the kingdom of God. 17 And he took the cup, and gave thanks, and said, Take this, and divide it among yourselves: 18 For I say unto you, I will not drink of the fruit of the vine, until the kingdom of God shall come.

The second meal, the meal of succession, is the meal held on the shore with Peter and the Apostles. The Passover/Eucharist was the meal of the soon-to-die suzerain. The meal of fish on the shore is the meal of the resurrected Last

---

[101] **THAT YOU MAY PROSPER** I Institute for Christian Economics I June 1987 I Pages 105-106.

Adam, the successor to the first Adam who was dead in sin and had lost his position of authority. Christ is now the successor, the Risen King of Glory. As the last Adam, we renew our oaths of fidelity to Him and His Kingdom every time we partake of the Eucharist. Because covenant oaths are self-maledictory oaths, many who did not understand the seriousness of this died when they partook in an unworthy manner, according to Paul in 1 Corinthians 11:30. When I first wrote this book, I wrote that it was Peter who was the successor, but this cannot be because Peter is nowhere identified as the Last Adam, and Adam is the key figure in God's covenant. If God had meant Peter to be the Last Adam and head over the family of man, He would have somewhere clearly specified this. What we do have clearly specified in Scripture is the link between the first Adam, and Christ who is the Last Adam.

Notice also how many of the Old Covenant congregation's rituals pull through to the New Covenant. The covenant cutting ritual of circumcision becomes baptism. The Passover Meal becomes the Eucharist. The high priest continues in the Great High Priest who is now a priest forevermore after the order of Melchizidek. The headship over the people of God by twelve tribes of Israel is replaced by the twelve Apostles.

This is the reality of covenant continuity. God established a family on earth, a people for Himself. He ordained a worship for them. There was no idea of there being any other place where God was to be properly worshiped according to the pattern He gave Moses. There was no idea that any of the pagan tribes around national Israel were somehow an acceptable form of worship. There was one visible congregation, the qāhēl, the Church.

In the Parable of the Wicked Husbandmen, the congregation of God, national Israel, is the husbandman of the vineyard, represented by the chief priests and the Pharisees who understood the parable was about them. There is change in the vineyard but its properties remain the same. The only thing that happens is that it is put under a new representative authority.

182

For a thousand years, it was a given that there was but one Church. There was no esoteric Calvinist idea of an invisible Church consisting only of true believers. There were not thirty thousand plus independent bodies laying claim to being the Church. Now Sutton adheres to a definition which says that the true Church is found wherever there are found true believers.

I simply cannot believe he would say this with a straight face. It violates every one of the principles of a covenant in some way. There is no single transcendent body which speaks for God, no single hierarchical and representational authority, no ethics because the understanding of ethics is fluid from assembly to assembly, no oaths/sanctions because to whom in true representative authority do you make them, and no continuity among the assemblies that have sprung up out of nowhere, unconnected to the past. Protestantism is a visible violation of all five points of the eternal covenant as regards the earthly congregation. This is presuppositional blindness at its worst.

Finally, I must challenge Bishop Sutton to show me the continuity of his own Episcopalian assembly. Please show me an unbroken line of visible representative authority which was handed down from generation to generation. That is what covenant continuity is – the handing down of authority from one generation to the next. Rome severed their unity with the Church when they began to teach that which ecumenical councils had condemned. Luther and Calvin and all who followed in their footsteps did the same thing. How do you possibly speak of covenant succession and not see that _only_ the Orthodox Church has the unbroken line of apostolic authority as the visible representative authority of God on earth?

SUMMARY

The Church is the congregation of God's people. It began in the wilderness and has continued to this very day as a visible body where God's established worship and sacrifices for sin are offered. When the nation to whom it was given rejected the One Who came as their Suzerainty King and killed Him, the congregation was taken from their oversight and put under a new authority. That change was symbolized by Jesus appointing the twelve Apostles to take the place of the twelve tribal heads of Israel. Jesus foretold this removal of covenant privilege in Matthew 21: 33-46, warned the Jews in Jerusalem of the coming covenant curse to fall on them in AD 70, and the hand of God tore the veil of the Temple apart, desecrating the Holiest of All and making it unfit for further use, thus ending the covenant.

All of these signs point to the change in representative authority on earth, an authority still visible in the Orthodox Church. The Reformers unknowingly but rightly make the case that the Roman Catholic Church lost that representative authority given to Peter and the Apostles. There is neither indication in scripture nor warrant to believe that the succession of authority would ever stop in the Orthodox Church – because of the eternal Yom Kippur that is offered to keep the Church in covenant with God. It is because of the eternal Yom Kippur that the Church – one, holy, *catholic,* [102] and apostolic – continues throughout the ages towards eternity. It is the same Church that began with Moses and was finalized as the congregation of God's people under the New Covenant to be the Church forevermore. As Orthodox believers, it is our hope and prayer that the Church at Rome would come to her senses, realize that she has broken her union with the Church of the first thousand years of Christianity, and return to the fold. Let us all pray for that union to be restored.

---

[102]

You must remember that the word "catholic" means universal. St.Vincent of Lerins clarified what it means to hold to the Catholic faith. It is that which has been believed at all times, by all people, and in all places. The invention of new dogmas, unknown to the Early Church, places the Roman Catholic Church outside the boundaries of this universal faith. This is why I had to leave for the faith once delivered to the Apostles.

RESISTENCE IS FUTILE –
I JOIN THE FAMILY

I am not a professional theologian. All I desired to do when I first wrote this book was to talk about some of the covenant principles which helped me to find the ancient and historic Christian faith – also known as the catholic, or "universal" (*katholicos*) faith. My special desire was to use the covenant to cover a couple of doctrines which Protestants find quite bothersome and inexplicable. For most Protestants, it takes a long time to overcome their prejudices against the many apostolic beliefs which I have written about. These are subjects that I, too, had to wrestle with on my journey to the Church. I hope that my explanations have given some reasonable and biblically based food for thought. They are the thoughts and ideas I would share with anyone over a cup of coffee.

Now I believe I have finalized my journey. What began in an honest decision, thinking that I was joining the Church which has existed from the beginning, has modified as I have come to understand that when the Roman Catholic Church left the unity of belief with Orthodoxy, they threw away being part of the united Church.

Here is what I originally wrote before entering communion with the Roman Catholic Church:

My own personal journey began in the same way that all journeys do: a small incident started me on the path of investigating the Catholic Church in a futile attempt to prove what Catholics believe is a load of hogwash. It may be the conversion of a friend, sometimes a particular verse of scripture, or a comment made by an associate which begins a non-Catholic down the path towards the Catholic faith, usually in an aggressively confrontational mode. In my case, it was an innocent looking link on a web site which began my trek Home.

The link took me to a Catholic forum where a number of people were regularly engaging in the noble practice of apologetics. Although I found the posts interesting, I was sure that these people were in deep error and in need of my expertise as a Calvinist to save their souls. So in I charged, full of Calvinist fire and brimstone for these poor, deluded, papist wretches, who obviously needed to hear from someone who understood the Bible properly.

They were totally unimpressed.

They answered my objections with clear and concise reasoning and backed them with scripture. I went away from that little meeting with a question ringing in my head over and over and over: if the Church is meant to be the pillar and ground of truth, and in being that, teach the truth of God to the nations, how can an invisible Church do that? Furthermore, how can a Church which is splintered into thousands of differing sects provide a uniform answer? How does this mess called Protestantism actually speak with one voice about one truth? These were nettlesome questions, made even more provoking to me as

I realized that in the Old Testament there had only been one congregation on earth where the sacrifices for sin and the word of God from prophets resided. How then could there be various competing bodies all claiming to be God's one, true Church? If there was a single physical body on earth in the Old Testament by which God spoke to the nations, how could God leave the earth bereft of a similar single voice of truth in the New Covenant? That made no sense at all.

I spent the next year and a half in study more intense than when I had been in school. I seemed to be reading all the time, and reading everything I could find that was suggested to me. Everything I considered as I read was put through the grid of the covenant of God. To my surprise, Catholic theology fit! The idea of a single body which is the covenant kingdom fit. The idea of baptismal regeneration fit! The idea of the Eucharist as the covenant meal of renewal fit!

Intrigued, I dove in deeper. I began to buy books. I joked one day with my new Internet friends that if anyone were to come in and look over my bookshelves, they would immediately ask me where I was keeping my Rosary. I also laughingly admitted that my buying of apologetic books was strange behavior indeed for someone who was determined to not go to Rome. I had recently changed to a Reformed Episcopalian assembly which was using a conservative and high liturgical rite. I was convinced, by a friend who had preceded me there from the PCA, that this was indeed the real Catholic Faith of the first century. Going to Rome? No. I was quite content where I was.

That lasted all of six months. I studied the issue of the Eucharist and valid priestly orders and came to understand that the Anglican break with Rome invalidated the priesthood of England. As a result of reading the Early Fathers, I also came to disagree with the position of this body on the Eucharist, for while it is clear that the Early Fathers, even St. Augustine, regarded the elements as truly the Body and Blood of Christ, my Episcopalian body taught an almost but not quite Real Presence. And that simply was not good enough for me. It was the Eucharist which had been driving my interest ever since I read Dr. Michael

Horton's defense of sacrament as means of grace some two years before. Even as a Presbyterian, once I had read that article I began to refer to the elements as the Body and Blood of the Lord, not understanding the issue of valid orders. When I found out that the historic understanding of the Early Fathers was not shared by the assembly I was attending, I became very perturbed. I wanted out, but was not ready for Rome or the Pope yet. But I was ready for the Eucharist.

When I finally figured out the familial relationship of the covenant, in no small part thanks to the wonderful books and tapes of our brother Scott Hahn, I was ready to move. Not quite ready to send prayers to our Blessed Mother, but I understood the concepts I have presented in this book in a germinal way and they were opening the doors of the Vatican and inviting me to come across the Tiber and enter my spiritual Home. In June of 2000 I began a series of catechumen's classes at St. Ann's Byzantine Catholic Church. I had a fascination with Eastern liturgy and worship, especially since they sang so much and I love to sing! The classes began with Christ's passion and took me through the history of the Church from Pentecost onward. We studied history and then moved right into doctrine and Eastern spirituality.

Now I faced a real and serious conflict. My sons were serving as acolytes at the Reformed Episcopalian Church we were attending. I would go to early service there, and then beat feet across town to attend Liturgy at St. Ann's. During one particular Liturgy, I thought I heard the voice of the Lord speak to my heart and tell me that this was where He wanted me to be. No argument from me! I was already a member in my heart. As far as I was concerned, the Easter Vigil couldn't come fast enough!!

To compound my problem, with the approach of summer, the service times were changing and I would be only able to attend one church. I cared deeply for the wonderful people in the Episcopal church, but my heart was completely at home at St. Ann's. Oh, what to do? What to do?

I spoke with Fr. John Tragillio at Seven Sorrows RC Church in Middletown. He listened to me with great interest and then simply said,

"Don't be in a hurry. God isn't. He will get you where He wants you to be in His own time. Just relax and enjoy the trip"

In retrospect, some of the best advice I ever got. I put it all on the Lord's shoulders in prayer and left it to Him. It wasn't five weeks later that I had the chance to talk with Fr. Heckert at the Episcopalian church. Bless his heart, he was not at all surprised. He had been bringing in a great deal of literature on praying the Rosary and other Catholic practices and had seen my great interest in this. When I explained my dilemma to him, he replied with great grace that if this was where I was called to, then I must go for the safety of my soul. Seeing that his parish had less than twenty five members and he was trying desperately to build it up as a mission parish, this was indeed an example of great grace on his part.

With the blessing of Fr. Heckert and an ever growing desire to learn more and more of the ancient and historical Christian faith as found in the Catholic Church, I severed myself from the Reformed Episcopalian body and began to be more seriously involved in learning the rites and rituals, the glory and beauty that is Eastern Catholic worship.

As with Scott Hahn, it was the covenant and my study of it which kept me heading home to the faith catholic. When one understands God's eternal covenant properly, other beliefs simply do not fit it. I found myself more and more intrigued with the Catholic Faith as the pieces fell into place one by one.

I found myself, like many catechumens, literally hungering to receive our Lord in the Blessed Eucharist. For me, Holy Saturday couldn't come fast enough. Yet, at the same time, the closer I came, the more the old doubts began to ooze through to the surface of my mind and bother me. For most converts, this time, especially during Lent, can be emotionally wrenching. They are not helped by well meaning friends and relatives who try to reason the catechumen out of his decision. I decided that it would be best for me to leave my discussions on the Internet with non-Catholics and concentrate my mind on the study of apologetic *materials. This indeed gave me some relief and intention to press forward with my conversion to the faith.*

After the Great Paschal celebration was over, I wrote to all my Internet friends who had been cheering me on and praying for me. Here is my description to them of my Holy Saturday:

Beloved in Christ!!
CHRIST IS RISEN!!
CHRISTOS VOSKRESE!!

From Great Saturday Stichera:
Today Hades tearfully sighs: "Would that I had not received Him who was born of Mary, for He came to me and destroyed my power. He broke my bronze gates and, being God, delivered those I had been holding captive" Glory to your cross and resurrection, O Lord!"

Warm greetings of joy on this day of our Lord's glorious Resurrection! I have been asked for a blow by blow account of my conversion weekend. I gladly and with great joy comply.

On Friday evening we had Solemn Vespers in which the tomb of Christ was brought forward before the Iconostasis. After the opening hymns and prayers, the priest led a the congregation around the church three times, holding aloft with two other priests, the icon sheet of the Crucified Christ. This was brought back in and placed atop the tomb. Around the tomb were massive amounts of lilies and flowers with three candles on large brass stands on both sides. Upon dismissal, each member of the congregation came forward on our knees and venerated the icon of His Crucifixion. After dismissal and until Saturday Vespers, people took turns guarding the tomb for one hour shifts. My turn came on Saturday at 4 PM. I spent the day, as much as possible within the confines of family responsibilities, reading and meditating upon the Crucifixion and my sins which sent our beloved Savior to the Cross.

At 5 PM, the catechumens gathered for final instructions. The service began in the nave with the recitation of vows to follow Christ, renunciation of the devil and his works, and our vows of fidelity to Holy Mother Church, the Holy Father, and the ordinary Magisterium. Then we were led into the sanctuary.

There were three catechumens who were baptized, in this case, by the threefold pouring of water over their heads in the name of the Father, the Son, and the Holy Spirit. Then we put on white robes and we were all chrismated with the Oil of Joy. I cannot begin to describe the beauty of the fragrance of this oil. It is rose oil and the scent is lovely. The three catechumens who were baptized were then marched three times around the table where the baptismal water and the oil of joy lay while we sang *"All who have been baptized into Christ have put on Christ"*.

Then the moment came which I have longed for. We closed the service with the Eucharist and I received Christ in this very special Sacrament. I would love to say to you that I saw angels and heard the heavenly choir, (you wouldn't believe how I had this event built up in my mind!) but it was a quite regular reception. As I told my godfather later, *"It is not the feelings that matter regarding this. It is the faith that I truly believe that this is the Son of God made present on the altar"*

We then received small crosses to wear and each one of us was given a lovely icon of Christ. I shall be having mine blessed on the altar next weekend for the required forty days.

My oldest daughter attended the ceremony, for which I was very thankful. Afterwards, my godfather, who is quickly becoming my best friend, had a chance to answer her questions regarding the altar the iconostasis, and the icons. I drove her home and got back just in time for the Resurrection Matins, which began at nine o'clock.

Having been initiated into the one, holy, catholic, and apostolic Church of our Lord, I joined the choir for the evening service. After the opening hymns, we processed the church carrying candles and the priest, stopping at the doors of the darkened church, proclaimed "Christ is risen." Every light in the church came on and the bells rung and we processed in with joy. The icon of the Crucifixion was removed from the tomb and the Paschal loaf was placed upon it. From there we sang the special hymns of the Resurrection and celebrated the Eucharist.

When the service was over, we all went into the church recreation hall for the blessing of the Paschal baskets. Each basket has the traditional meal in it consisting of:

Pascha - ("Paska") A sweet yeast bread rich in eggs, butter, etc. Symbolic of Christ Himself. Braid encircles the top, giving it a crown effect.

Ham - (Sunka -- "shoon-ka") Main dish because of its richness and symbolic of great joy and abundance of Easter.

Sausage - ("kolbasi") A spicy, garlicy sausage of pork products, indicative of God's favor and generosity.

Butter - (maslo - "ma-slo") Shaped into a figure of a lamb or small cross. This reminds us of the goodness of Christ that we should have toward all things.

Eggs - (Pisanki - "pi-sun-ki") Hard boiled eggs brightly decorated with symbols and markings made with beeswax. Indicative of new life and resurrection.

Cheese - (hrudku - "hrood-ka") A custard type cheese shaped into a ball haveing a rather bland but sweet taste indicative of the moderation that Christians should have in all things. Also creamed cheese is placed in a small dish and both are decorated with symbols made out of cloves.

Horseradish - (Chrin - "Khrin") Symbolic of the passion of Christ still in our midst by sweeted with some sugar because of the resurrection.

Salt - ("sol") A condiment necessary for flavor reminding the Christian of this duty to others.

Today, after Resurrection Liturgy, I went to Ray and Marie's house for dinner. The food is every bit as wonderful as the description. The fellowship was warm and wonderful too. We had a room full of converts.

I must say that this has been the most meaningful Lenten and Paschal celebration I have ever had. It all came together for me when I sat down to dinner and looked upon all the food. For forty days we have fasted, reflecting upon our sins and how barren our lives were without Christ. And before me, was this *feast*, so very symbolic of the feast which Christ makes our life by His resurrection.

I have heard of converts who woke up in the morning a couple of months after their conversion and thought to themselves *"Omigosh. What have I done?"* Honestly, I didn't think or feel that at all. In fact, at liturgy this morning, I felt quite at home.

So that is my wonderful weekend. It was kind of tiring, kind of exhilarating, and kind of ordinary. But it will never be lived again.

This is not an end point. Today is the beginning. Now I face the rest of my life to grow more in Christ, to deepen my faith, to walk with the Lord in charity for my fellow man. St. Paul urges us:

Heb 12:1 Wherefore seeing we also are compassed about with so great a cloud of witnesses, let us lay aside every weight, and the sin which doth so easily beset us, and *let us run with patience the race that is set before us,* 2 Looking unto Jesus the author and finisher of our faith; who for the joy that was set before him endured the cross, despising the shame, and is set down at the right hand of the throne of God.

INDEED HE IS RISEN!!!
VOISTINU VOSKRESE!!!

And the joyous journey continues to this day.

As you can see, it was quite a struggle for me, a momentous journey which brought me much closer to the faith of the Apostles. For a considerable time, I felt at home, not understanding that the idea of being Orthodox in communion with Rome is simply an impossibility. My years in the Byzantine

Catholic Church showed me a faith which was, in many instances, less Orthodox and more Roman. I found it disconcerting, for instance, to go into a major BCC church in downtown Pittsburgh and hear the Rosary being played over loudspeakers. In this same church, there were gaping holes in the floor where the Iconostasis had been ripped out and was gone. I was more than once chided in coffee hour discussions for not holding to distinctive Roman dogmas as I attempted to live an Orthodox life while being in a Catholic church.

It all finally came to a head. I simply could not stand the conflict between what I was in my heart and what I was expected to be. On April 23rd of 2022, I was chrismated into the Orthodox Church in America. I had fervently desired this for three years, but there were impediments which held me back. After reading about one of Orthodoxy's revered saints – St. Paisios of Athos – I began praying to him and asking him to open the doors to Orthodoxy for me. It was not long before those impediments vanished. I guess you know who my patron saint is!

I realize that in this writing I may sound overly harsh in places toward the Roman Catholic Church. Please believe me when I say that I do not want to be the kind of Orthodox believer whose sole commitment to Orthodoxy is a profound hatred of and disrespect towards Roman Catholics and their church. It is my hope that I may continue to have good friendships with my many Roman Catholic friends and pray from the heart that the differences between Orthodoxy and the Roman Church can be worked out so that we are once again united. Many have expressed this desire. May I add my prayers to theirs.

There are many in that church who have done wonderful things and have written beautifully about the Christian faith. I close this chapter with the writing of one of them:

A CLOSING WORD FROM THOMAS MERTON

"What is serious to men is often very trivial in the sight of God. What in

God might appear as "play" is perhaps what He Himself takes most seriously. At any rate the Lord plays and diverts Himself in the garden of His creation, and if we could let go of our own obsession with what we think is the meaning of it all, we might be able to hear His call and follow Him in His mysterious, cosmic dance. We do not have to go very far to catch echoes of that game, and of that dancing. When we are alone on a starlit night; when by chance we see the migrating birds in autumn descending on a grove of junipers to rest and eat; when we see children in a moment of when they are really children; when we know love in our own hearts; or when, like the Japanese poet Basho we hear an old frog land in a quiet pond with a solitary splash – at such times the awakening, the turning inside out of all values, the "newness," the emptiness and the purity of vision that make themselves evident, provide a glimpse of the cosmic dance.

For the world and time are the dance of the Lord in emptiness. The silence of the spheres is the music of a wedding feast. The more we persist in misunderstanding the phenomena of life, the more we analyze them out into strange finalities and complex purposes of our own, the more we involve ourselves in sadness, absurdity and despair. But it does not matter much, because no despair of ours can alter the reality of things, or stain the joy of the cosmic dance which is always there. Indeed, we are in the midst of it, and it is in the midst of us, for it beats in our very blood, whether we want it to or not. Yet the fact remains that we are invited to forget ourselves on purpose, cast our awful solemnity to the winds and join in the general dance." (Conjectures of a Guilty Bystander published in 1966 by Doubleday & Co.)

Some Answers to Common Questions

Because we have common apostolic roots, many of the beliefs of the Roman Catholic church are shared with Orthodoxy under slightly different forms. For instance, while we reject the notion of the Immaculate Conception, we speak of Mary as the immaculate and sinless one. With this in mind, I would like to respond to some common objections which Protestants have against our mutual apostolic understanding of the Christian faith.

1. *"The idea of Purgatory insults the work of Christ. How can you say that Christ's work didn't take away all of our sins?"*

In Orthodoxy, we do not believe in a place called Purgatory, but we do understand the need for a final cleansing of the soul before it begins the everlasting, ever-deepening journey into the love of God.

I can say that Christ's work didn't take away all our sins because the idea of God making a legal declaration of not guilty (forensic justification or imputed righteousness) which wipes away all your sins – past, present, and future – is a theological legal fantasy, an idea concocted by the Reformers which was simply unknown prior to Luther and Calvin. If this were true, the Church would have recognized this teaching in its early years and done away with confession and the priesthood, since there would be no need for either.

Entrance into a covenant relationship involves oaths, and sanctions for the breaking of those oaths. In a relationship, the persons in the relationship deal with the reality of who the other truly is. Just like human relationships, it is possible, after making those marriage vow and entering the covenant of marriage, to offend your spouse. It is even possible to so destroy the relationship that it ends. In the same manner, it is possible to break our relationship with God through our sin. Forgiveness of this is not automatic. Unlike Luther's idea of imputed righteousness, we do not get covered by a snow white blanket of Christ's righteousness. There is no legal paperwork in heaven which God looks upon when we sin and says "That's alright. I already forgave him for that." God deals with us as we are, and if we are in a state of sin, He sees it.

Sin is putting something else between us and our love for Him. It is an attitude of the heart which needs to be worked on to change. No legal declaration will make you a different person. Only the grace of God found in the Sacraments of Confession (covenant renewal) followed by the Eucharist (covenant renewal meal) will do that to you. This is why God called the sins of national Israel "adultery" in the book of Hosea. That is a very personal term which indicates a loss of love for Him. It is giving the intimacy of our love to another who does not deserve it. Our sin does the same thing to us. If we sin, He sees that sin and the condition of our soul as it loves something else other than Him. No amount of legal paperwork is going to change what we are inside. We need to receive His cleansing and forgiveness so that the sin and its effect on our souls is removed. Left to fester, sin has a way of drawing us further and further from the love we are supposed to have for our Lord.

Now suppose we fail to get to the confessional before we die? What do we do with the sin upon our souls? That unconfessed sin is something I am still clinging to because I love it. Purgation after death will not only deal with the sin that remains, cleansing my soul, it will make an ontological change in me so that I am fit to enter into the complete self-giving of love to God which is heaven.

Here is a nice analogy I really like: just as fire meets wood and changes the wood into itself, so we meet God, and the fiery and passionate love of God changes us into beings like unto Himself. Remember, in Orthodoxy, our view of soteriology is all about being (ousia) and not so much about law-keeping. Purgation after death is that event when all that is still not like God is changed to be like Him. This change into God-likeness goes on throughout the life of a believer. Purgation is the final removal of all that didn't get changed, a cleansing from all the habits of our "old man" in Adam.

Oh, and one other thing. Purgation after death is *not* a second chance at heaven! I cannot tell you how many times I get this objection indignantly thrown at me. It is the final cleansing for those whom God has found to be faithful covenant keeping children. Those who have ignored the covenant, spurned the family, cared not for God, and done evil, will find that they are disinherited from all that was set aside for them by Christ as the Head of all mankind. Knowing what they could have enjoyed, but spurned by their taste for wickedness here on earth, will be torment for them.

2. *"The Bible teaches that men are either the 'children of the devil' or the 'children of God.' This proves that Calvinist are right to say that all men are, by their birth, children of the devil until they are born again as the children of God."* *Total depravity is a true teaching.*

To use the term children implies fatherhood – the act of creation of life and the relationship therein – from someone. In the idea of procreation, the creating of life – the devil doesn't do that. I have yet to see one text which states that he who is the giver of death can somehow give life. The idea that somehow, a child born in this world is automatically a child of the evil one – which would imply either procreation or relationship – is terribly wrong thinking. Therefore, this can only refer to covenant headship in some way. Remember, the term father can refer to a position of covenant headship.

When Adam sinned in the Garden, he *made a covenant* with the evil one by the force of believing and acting in faith upon the words of death. The covenant headship, therefore, was transferred from the legitimate family head, the Eternal God, to the usurper who had now intruded into the family. Adam's act of eating was ultimately an act of faith in the words of the wicked one and allegiance to him. It put Adam and the whole human race under the false headship of the evil one. This is why there had to come One Who was outside this covenant relationship – i.e. born of a virgin and therefore not of a man's seed and the covenant corruption in that lineage – and who could not only release men from death by His death, but would establish Himself as the Last Adam under the headship of the Eternal Father.

Calvinists love to turn in their Bibles to the passage in John 8 where Christ scolds the Pharisees and tells them that they are *"of your Father the devil, for his deeds ye do."* This is their proof text, referred to numerous times in debates and arguments, that men and women are naturally of the devil and therefore have nothing to do with God at all. But they miss the qualifier in that verse which says *". . . for his works ye do"*.

By the doing of the works of the wicked one, the Pharisees made a false covenant with the devil. Remember, the Pharisees were of the covenant God had made with Abraham. They were, therefore, circumcised children of the covenant and rightly called themselves children of Abraham. Now if they were of the circumcision, and had made covenant with God through circumcision which made them part of the kingdom family of God, how then could Christ call them children of the devil as He did?

Isa 28:15 "Because ye have said, We have made a covenant with death, and with hell are we at agreement; when the overflowing scourge

shall pass through, it shall not come unto us: for we have made lies our refuge, and under falsehood have we hid ourselves: 16 Therefore thus saith the Lord GOD, Behold, I lay in Zion for a foundation a stone, a tried stone, a precious corner stone, a sure foundation: he that believeth shall not make haste. 17 Judgment also will I lay to the line, and righteousness to the plummet: and the hail shall sweep away the refuge of lies, and the waters shall overflow the hiding place. 18 And *your covenant with death* shall be disannulled, and your agreement with hell shall not stand;"

Perfect description of the Pharisees. Just as Adam, made a false covenant with death by his action in the Garden, so also the Pharisees made a covenant with death by their actions. By doing so, they refused the headship of the Eternal Father and by their acts put themselves willingly under the headship of the Evil One, even though they did not recognize this. They had given themselves over to lies and falsehood. They made covenant with the Evil One. But that does not mean that all of mankind has willingly done so simply by being born.

The other problem is that if this supposition is true, how then does the Bible speak of righteous Abel, righteous Noah and all the other men and women of the Bible who are called righteous before the coming of Christ? How can the Bible possibly refer to these people as righteous when Calvinist dogma states that they are dead in sin and therefore all that they do is evil?

3. *The Holy Spirit led me to become* _____ . *(Fill in your favorite and preferred religion here.)*

I want to keep this in the context of covenant structure again. This is simply impossible if you have understood the analogies I have referred to in this book. The Trinitarian Godhead has one covenant and one family relationship. This covenant of love was extended to Creation by means of establishing a priest/king representative on earth who was the son of God and who was to establish his family on earth to be a congregation of priest/kings under his federal authority as head of Creation. This whole structure implies singularity and unity of family, not the fractured mess we see in Christendom today.

Protestantism violates all five covenant principles.

1. Transcendence – There is no sense of the greater offering blessings to the lesser in Protestantism.

2. Hierarchy – The sense of a single, visible authority, which is the Church, speaking with the authority of God and on His behalf is destroyed.

3. Ethics – There is no set standard of ethics from one assembly to the next. Each assembly has their own idea of what is sin and what is not.

4. Oaths/sanctions – Ritual oath making to enter the covenant is destroyed, especially in Anabaptist congregations.

5. Succession – The Orthodox faith has a traceable lineage of succession from the Apostles, thus succession of covenant and covenant authority.

In short, the idea of the Holy Spirit leading someone to oppose the very principles of the covenant and covenant family upon which the Church is built is nothing short of preposterous! My feeling is that an awful lot of people have mistaken their happy feelings for the leading of the Holy Spirit – with disastrous results to the unity of Christendom.

4. *"But I don't need a priest, I can go directly to God and ask forgiveness."*

Since you are Protestant and most likely sola scriptura, I will respond by saying, Show me where it says that in the Bible. What I find in the scriptures is the principle that God established a visible, representative covenant authority (Principle 2 – Hierarchy) by which we would be related to Him and through whom we would receive the blessings of covenant faithfulness.

More than that though, rejection of a visible authority established by God is rejection of God Himself. This is no small matter. The attitude expressed towards a symbol is directed at the reality that the symbol represents. Thus we understand that when a man burns the American flag, while in essence he is burning a colored piece of cloth, he is expressing a true hatred for the country which that flag represents. The same is true of the priesthood. It is not the priest you reject – it is God Who ordained the priesthood as the means of covenantally representing Him through the ministration of the Sacraments of the Covenant. The fact is that just like in the Garden of Eden, God says "Do it this way" and you, in your actions, say "No, I want to do it _my_ way." And as we have seen through the sad centuries of mankind – our way is always the wrong way.

5. _"Why would you want me to become Orthodox when we see priests molesting children and the Orthodox churches fighting with one another?"_

Because regardless of the evil people in the Church, the Church is still the Church. Furthermore, the Church is not defined by those who do not keep Her moral teachings. This problem didn't start in recently. If you read St. Paul's epistles to the various house congregations which composed the Church, he was constantly dealing with a variety of sins: incestuous relationships, arguments, factions, drunkenness at the Lord's Table. Seeing that behavior, would you have refused to become a Christian back then as well?

Jesus taught us that the kingdom would be like a net filled with good and bad fish and a field filled with wheat and tares. The twelve men closest to Him constantly quarreled among themselves for positions of honor in the coming Kingdom. And one of them betrayed Him!

I am not inviting you to join bad Christians in their bad behavior. I am inviting you to enter the covenant family in which there is salvation from your own sins. Take your eyes off the very few bad priests who caused the recent scandal. Don't look at the multitude of lazy and indifferent Orthodox (and Catholics). They are not your goal. Christlikeness is your goal and the Church is here to help you achieve this. Prove to yourself, by the reading of quality

202

apologetic materials, that the Orthodox has the fullness of the apostolic faith of the first centuries. Look at the lives of the saints if you wish to see the goal for our lives! My invitation to you to join the Church is an invitation to join those of us who struggle every day to live lives of holiness and help us show Christ to a world hungering to see Him!

And by the way, the scandal of child molestation was almost unknown in Orthodoxy. It is a problem in the Roman Catholic church and Protestantism.

7. *"Your church is a sexist and misogynist organization that mistreats women and has done so since its beginning."*

I honestly have to wonder what history of the world that you have been reading if you make a statement like this. The history of the world prior to the Christian faith was utterly misogynist. The beginnings of Christianity found a Roman empire in which the treatment of women represented the standard degradation of them which occurred throughout the world. Here is some information from a female writer on this subject:

"For today, let's look at some mores that exhibit the status of women in Jewish and surrounding cultures at the time Jesus walked the earth (many of these status-related norms are still with us today in various parts of the world).

Female babies are of low worth: In past and present non-Christian cultures, female worthlessness is widespread. Female babies were commonly the victims of infanticide. While that continues today, in places where ultrasound is available many more female fetuses are aborted than male fetuses (especially in China and India). Christians do not value females less than males and do not abort or kill female babies. (See a recent article: A woman cost rs 30,000, a buffalo is 70,000.)

Polygyny and divorce: Polygyny was permitted though not very common in ancient Israel; it was relatively common elsewhere. In Greece, a man had one wife but he also had a legal mistress (so, essentially, a 2nd wife). Polygyny was not approved by God, though there are a number of instances of it recorded in the Bible. The NT clearly reiterates God's will that one man be married to one woman; polygyny is not allowed in Christianity. A man could divorce his wife easily in ancient Israel, but the NT does not allow for this.

Complete control of wife and children by father or husband: In Rome, fathers had total control over family members and a husband had absolute power over his wife; he could sell a daughter to her future husband. All these powers became illegal some years after Christianity became legal in Rome (374/313). Women also were granted the right to own property and have guardianship of their own children. In Greece, wives had segregated quarters and could not visit with male guests of her husband's in her own home. As in ancient Israel, women in Greece were not to speak in public. Women simply had a very low status in Greece and ancient Israel, and in Israel at the time of Christ, women's legal witness was virtually non-existent. This changed with Christ's work and will get more attention in future articles.

Clitoridectomy: The removal of the female clitoris, and often other genital parts, is a common practice in many African countries (and is found in countries where Africans have immigrated to). This is condemned and outlawed in Christian-based countries.

Binding feet, China: In order to be more attractive to men, girls used to have their feet bound so that they remained "small." The fact is, the foot only became very disfigured and it often became severely infected. Because of Christian missionary pressure in the 19th century, the Chinese government outlawed the practice of female foot binding in 1912." [103]

The real complaint being fielded here is that the Church does not A.) permit women to be ordained, and B.) will not go along with what has come to be called "female reproductive freedom," meaning abortion and contraception.

The simple fact of the matter is this: the world was created to follow a divine pattern of the heavenly. First, God the Father identifies Himself as male. The use of this gender in describing God causes us to seek proper analogies in the world of human beings in which we live. God wants us to look at an earthly father to understand something of His relationship to mankind.

A. A father is the giver of life. He creates life by placing his seed within the woman, who is the nurturer of life. God as giver of life created man with a body that gives life, thus becoming an icon of Himself. As the woman, so is Creation, which received the life giving movements of God in Genesis and brought forth life abundantly. This why the Church is also called "Holy *Mother* the Church." It is because She, the Church, receives life from the Father in the form of the Eucharist, and in turn, gives this true meat and drink, along with instruction and guidance, to Her children to nurture and care for them.

B. The priest, when giving the Eucharist, places that which gives life into the receptive body of those who come forward to commune with God through Christ. Thus, a female, who is a receiver of life, cannot possibly be an accurate picture of male life giving. To be female is to be a receiver and nurturer of life, and it is something that women do exceedingly well, much better than a man can do. It is a shame that women are not being taught to celebrate their nurturing abilities by feminists who are jealous of male leadership.

C. As the Creator of life, it is impossible that God would sanction the sterility of contraception or the death of children. It is the false and demonic

---

[103] **Christian Views and Treatment of Women: Jesus Elevates Woman |
Victoria Priest, Christian Apologetics Examiner | http://www.examiner.com/
article/christian-views-and-treatment-of-women-jesus-elevates-woman**

pagan gods who are the creators of death. From the earliest recordings of history, the annals of mankind's pagan religions are filled with human sacrifice, and women were much more sacrificed than men. Wherever Christianity went, it put a stop to these barbaric practices and taught that women were to be treated with the dignity due to them as children of God.

The Orthodox faith elevates a woman to a position of honor which is even above that of the angels. We address Her as our Queen and Mother, and treat her with the utmost respect. In the beautiful Orthodox Liturgy of St. John Chrysostom, we sing of the Theotokos, the God-bearer, who is "More honorable than the cherubim, and beyond compare, more glorious than the seraphim, who a virgin gave birth to God the word, you truly the Theotokos we magnify."

Our Church is filled with nuns and religious sisters. If you are ever around a bunch of Orthodox or Catholic believers and a nun enters the area, watch and see the respect which is given her. Some of the most holy saints in our faith are women. Women fill important positions in the Church as teachers, professors of theology, and administrators.

What we do not do with women is what the world still does with them: teach them that promiscuity is acceptable and then, when they are pregnant, entice them to kill their children. Enslave them in sex-trafficking rings. Make pornographic videos and pictures of them which teach young men that a woman is nothing more than an object for sexual gratification rather than a person made in the image of God and to be treated with dignity. I find it bizarre that feminists will proclaim that allowing their bodies to be used by men, many times whom they will never see again, is somehow a statement of liberation.

Dear women of the world, when will you realize that the Church wants you to experience a life of being loved by men, honored as mothers, and treated with dignity? What you want is not dignity, it is slavery. Ask any woman who has had an abortion or suffered being treated as an object in a non-Christian culture.

8. *"What about the doctrine of election? How can you say that Calvinists are wrong about this when it is right in the Bible?"*

They are wrong because they have not understood the context in which St. Paul spoke. The context of the elect is most often referred to in the book of Romans. This is the favorite passage of most Calvinists. But they do not understand the context, not only of this chapter, but of the Bible as a whole.

In Romans, Paul is speaking of a certain class of people who will be saved from the destruction which is to come in 70 AD when Jerusalem is destroyed by the armies of the Roman general Titus. We see Christ speaking of this event and warning people of its immanence in places such as Matthew chapters 23 to 25.

Why are some of the Jews elect and some are not? It because of the hardness of their hearts, the choice they have made that like Pharaoh, they have passed the point of no return and no longer can hear.

Matthew 13:15 "For this people's heart is waxed gross, and their ears are dull of hearing, and their eyes they have closed; lest at any time they should see with their eyes, and hear with their ears, and should understand with their heart, and should be converted, and I should heal them."

Do you see whose fault this is? It is not God's fault, for He came to His own and His own received Him not. They have closed their eyes, their ears are dull of hearing, and they have no understanding because they have done this. Therefore, they are not elect to avoid the coming destruction.

Matthew 13:16 But blessed are your eyes, for they see: and your ears, for they hear.

These are the elect. And why are they elect? Because they listen with open hearts, heed the word, and act upon it. They believe Christ and seek to obey Him, unlike the Pharisees. The reason why some listened and some did not, which goes on even today, is a mystery of God's providence. They will be saved from the destruction of Jerusalem and the horrors that fell upon that city. The tern election is not about the whole human race. It cannot be because it contradicts numerous other verses in the Bible which speak about the will of God being to have mercy upon all and to save all. [104] To say that the doctrine of election as found in Calvinism is true creates a God who is schizophrenic and has two different wills, one to have mercy on all and one to save only the elect. When I was in Protestantism, I was told that the Bible could not contradict itself.

The idea of a God who elects some to salvation and others to damnation creates a conflict in the Godhead and in the Scriptures. Simply put, it cannot be true.

Election is a covenant oath/sanction response of God to the covenant breaking of the Jews. As I have shown earlier, covenant breaking results in bringing a covenant curse upon yourself. This is what the Pharisees, and all unbelieving Jews who followed them, did to themselves. They brought the curse of covenant breaking down upon their own heads. It was not God's doing – it was theirs!

---

[104] 1 Timothy 2:4; John 12:47; 1 Corinthians 15:22; Romans 11:32; 2 Corinthians 5: 14-15

MATTHEW 16, THE KEYS, AND THE CHURCH

There is a distressing and somewhat annoying habit of Roman Catholics to immediately jump to Matthew 16: 18-19 when involved in discussions which question the legitimacy of the papacy or the Roman Catholic church as being **the** Church. For them, these two verses establish both the papacy, and the Roman Catholic Church as the true church. I will post these verses and then tender my objections to them. I think they are misread, misunderstood, and those who lean on them are presuppositionally blinded by their desire for these verses to mean what they want to them to mean.

Matthew 16:18 And I say also unto thee, That thou art Peter, and upon this rock I will build my church; and the gates of hell shall not prevail against it. 19 And I will give unto thee the keys of the kingdom of heaven: and whatsoever thou shalt bind on earth shall be bound in heaven: and

whatsoever thou shalt loose on earth shall be loosed in heaven.

The gates of hell named in verse 18 are the assurance that for Roman Catholics that their church will not be overcome by evil. But they are seeing this all wrong. What are gates? Do gates attack and overcome the defenses of those they are attacking? Of course not! Gates are a defensive weapon to keep out something that is not wanted within a certain boundary:

Deuteronomy 28:52 And he shall besiege thee in all thy gates, until thy high and fenced walls come down, wherein thou trustedst, throughout all thy land: and he shall besiege thee in all thy gates throughout all thy land, which the LORD thy God hath given thee.

Deuteronomy 28 is a chapter in which both blessing and curse are spoken of to the people of Israel. Blessing if they keep covenant with God, but curse if they break their covenant vows. Notice what happens in verse 52. The gates cannot keep out the nation which comes to besiege Israel as part of the curse. Gates are defensive, not offensive. The promise of Christ in Matthew 16:18 is that when the Gospel goes forth into the world, beginning with Israel, the gates of hell which will try to keep the Gospel away from the people, will not prevail. The Church will move forward with the Gospel message and hell's gates will be unable to stop it.

Roman Catholics insist that this verse means that their church cannot teach error, but that is not at all the meaning. The Gospel will succeed in bringing people to God, no matter where it goes or what defenses against it are found.

"But what about Peter being given the keys to the Kingdom of Heaven? Surely that shows that he is the one who is in charge of the Church, since he alone is given the keys."

That sounds very plausible on the face of it, but there is a small detail that these folks have overlooked. The detail is this: what is the Kingdom of Heaven?

You see, this phrase is only found in Matthew's Gospel. This fact should immediately make you stop and question why. Why do we not find this in the Gospel of Luke or Mark? It is because it has a special meaning that only a Jew would understand. Remember, in studying the Bible, you must take into account not only the words at face value, but the context, the location, the intent, and the people who are being addressed. Jesus was addressing Jews in the Gospel of the Jews. That is what the Matthean Gospel is – the Gospel to, about, and for the Jews. Therefore, let's see how I, as a first-century Jew, would have understood this. What is the Kingdom of Heaven?

It appears that early Christians, much like those of today, did not think like first-century Jews when reading the Scriptures. For instance, when Jesus speaks of "heaven and earth," he is not speaking of this physical planet, nor the sky above us. Heaven and earth are a reference to the Temple.

"Jews did not always mean "the physical universe" when they spoke of heaven and earth together. In Jewish literature, the Temple was a portal connecting heaven and earth. They called it the "navel of the earth" and the "gateway to heaven" (Jub 8:19; 1 Enoch 26:1). Just like the Mesopotamian Tower in Genesis 11, the Temple connected God's realm to where humans lived.

To reflect this belief, the Jerusalem Temple had been built to look like a microcosm of the universe. We typically overlook how literally true the Temple hymn preserved in Psalm 78:69 is: "He built his sanctuary like the high heavens, like the earth, which he has founded forever." The actual holy place and most holy place inside the Temple building were constructed like earth and heaven. The courts outside represented the sea. I am not making this stuff up.

According to Josephus, two parts of the tabernacle were "approachable and open to all" but one was not. He explains that in so doing Moses "signifies the earth and the sea, since these two are accessible to all; but the third portion he reserved for God alone because heaven is inaccessible to men" (Ant. 3:181, cf. 3:123). The veil between the accessible and inaccessible parts of the Temple was designed to represent the entire material world during Jesus' day. Josephus and Philo agree that the veil was composed of four materials representing the four elements–earth, water, air, and fire (War 5:212-213; Ant. 3:138-144; Quaestiones in Exodum 2:85, cf. Mos 2:88). Heaven was beyond this material world. It was behind the curtain.

Outside the Temple's microcosm of "heaven and earth," the courts looked like the sea. Numbers Rabbah 13:19 records, "The court surrounds the temple just as the sea surrounds the world." In Talmudic tradition, Rabbis described how the inner walls of the Temple looked like waves of the sea (b. Sukk. 51b, b.B.Bat. 4a). From heaven and earth inside the temple, you looked out at the sea surrounding the world. Why? Ancients believed the earth had one giant land mass surrounded by sea. The temple reflected that cosmology. The accessible section of the Temple and the surrounding courts embodied both the land mass and sea believed to comprise the earth. The Most Holy Place was heaven where God's presence resided.

If we listen to Jesus in First-Century Israel, his prediction of "heaven and earth" passing away sounds like the destruction of Jerusalem and her Temple. The contemporary songs, writers, and architecture all make the connection between Jerusalem's Temple and "heaven and earth." Isaiah used the same language of "heaven and earth" to depict Jerusalem and her citizens in Isaiah 65:17-18.

"For behold, I create new heavens and a new earth and the former things will not be remembered or come to mind. But be glad and rejoice forever in what I create; For behold, I create Jerusalem for rejoicing and her people for gladness."

Isaiah is predicting the eventual reconstruction of Jerusalem after its destruction at the hands of invaders. He uses Hebrew parallelism to equate the creation of "new heavens and a new earth" with the restoration of Jerusalem. So Jesus isn't the first prophet to describe Jerusalem and her temple with grand language describing its theological significance. Jerusalem was the place where people encountered the presence of God on earth. The Temple is where heaven met earth." [105]

The Kingdom of Heaven is the Church! And what was the Church at the time of Jesus' ministry on earth. National Israel! We see this when St. Paul directly quotes Psalm 22:22 in Hebrews:

Hebrews 2:12 "Saying, I will declare thy name unto my brethren, in the midst of the church will I sing praise unto thee."

In Greek, the word is eclessia (ἐκκλησ ας), translated "church." It means "congregation or gathering," same word as לְהָק (qahal) in Hebrew. The Church is the earthly gathering of God's people in a distinct place, with distinct rites of worship, in a distinct building. There is no such thing as this nebulous idea of an invisible church, created by Protestants who wanted to soothe their consciences regarding their rebellion from Rome, who claimed to be the Church based on misinterpretation of Matthew 16. The keys are, I believe, to the gates of hell, which are holding the Jews in bondage to the Law and against the Gospel. The gates of hell will not be able to withstand the coming of the Gospel to the Jews at the hand of Peter.

But since Peter has more than one key, for what could be the rest? It is further interesting, and goes to prove my point quite well, that the Early Fathers felt that the key of David (Revelation 3:7, a text also used to prove Petrine primacy) actually had to do with interpretation of the Scriptures.

---

[105] Penley, "When Heaven and Earth Passed Away: Everything Changed." Para. 5–11.

The "keys" pertain to interpretative authority:

Origen in Book V, Chapter 4 of his commentary on Revelation and Book II, Chapter 4 of his commentary on the Gospel of John implies that "the key of David" pertains *to the interpreting of Scriptures*. This is an interpretation that the fathers all appear to share about "the key of David" specifically, other than Saint Irenaeus who simply states that the "key of David" was entrusted from the Father to the Son for judgement (A.H., Book IV, Chap 20, Par 2).

Saint Jerome (Letter 58, Par. 9) appears to see the keys not only in a sense akin to Origen, but also representative of *interpretative religious authority.* This is an interpretation somewhat analogous to Matthew Henry, who believed the keys were the power to preach the Gospel. We see both views fleshed out in the following sources:

John says in the Apocalypse: 'he who has the key of David, he who opens and no one shuts, and who shuts and no one opens.' This is the key held in the Law by the scribes and Pharisees who the Lord warns in the Gospel: 'Woe to you lawyers! who hold the key of the kingdom of heaven' (Luke 11:52). O you Pharisees, *who hold the keys to the kingdom* and do not believe in Christ who is the gate of the kingdom and the door, to you, indeed, the promise is made, but to us it is granted." **(Homily 66).**

[T]here are today who fancy themselves learned, yet the Scriptures are a sealed book to them, and one which they cannot open unless through Him who has the key of David, "he that openeth and no man shutteth; and shutteth and no man openeth." In the Acts of the Apostles the holy eunuch (or rather "man" for so the scripture calls him) when reading Isaiah he is asked by Philip "Understandest thou what thou readest?", makes answer:–"How can I except some man should guide me" **(Letter 53)?**

Saint Augustine, in passing, interprets the "keys" as such in one passage:
The Scribes then were they who professed the knowledge of the Law, and
to them belonged both the keeping and the studying, as well as also the
transcribing and the expounding, of the books of the Law. Such were they
whom our Lord Jesus Christ rebukes, because they have the keys of the
kingdom of heaven (Sermon 24, Par 1-2).

Saint Andrew of Caesarea has a similar interpretation:

His kingdom is called the key of David, for it is the symbol of authority.
The key is also the Holy Spirit, (the key) of both the book of Psalms and
every prophecy, through which the treasures of knowledge are opened (St
Andrew of Caesarea quoted in a Catena).

When Peter was sent to the Jews, he held two keys: one to open the gates
of hell and let the prisoners out, the second to open the interpretation of the
scriptures – the Old Testament – and show how Jesus the Christ is the promised
Messiah.

Remember, Peter is the Apostle to the Jews, while Paul was sent to the
Gentiles. Jesus is commissioning Peter, giving him the authority to open the gates
of hell and release those Jews imprisoned in their unbelief in the Messiah. Keys
are also a sign of authority. In Matthew 16, this commission is a special one for
Peter only. No other apostle is sent to the Jews but Peter. Two chapters later, we
see the same authority being given to all the disciples:

**Matthew 18:18 "Verily I say unto you, Whatsoever ye shall bind on
earth shall be bound in heaven: and whatsoever ye shall loose on earth shall
be loosed in heaven."**

One could perhaps say that at this point, the keys to the Kingdom of
Heaven were given to all the apostles, each to go to his assigned territory. For
instance, upon the diaspora, St. Thomas went to India and began to unlock the
gates of hell which held the Indian people in their idol worship and superstition.

This is why context is so very important when studying the Sacred
Scriptures. At this moment, Jesus is addressing the faith of the one who is to be

the Apostle to the Jews. It is in the specifically Jewish Gospel of Matthew. When the covenant relationship with national Israel ended (Hebrews 8:13) in AD 70 upon the destruction of Jerusalem, Peter's work was over and the keys were returned to Christ.

Unfortunately, this is what I missed when I left Protestantism for the Byzantine Catholic Church, a church in communion with the errors of Rome. Had I put more thought into it, I would have realized that only the Last Adam could replace the first Adam. Adam, a man, was covenant head to all mankind and over all creation. Therefore, another man is required to take the covenant headship which Adam forfeited. Only the man, Christ Jesus, fills that position perfectly. To say that the pope is the head of the Church is to usurp that position which rightly belongs to Christ. Furthermore, there is no document anywhere in which the Bishop of Rome is given the important covenant title The Last Adam.

This is not to say that Roman Catholics are not Christians or that they do not have valid sacraments. It is simply an explanation of why I disagree with their apologetic proofs that the Church of Rome is exclusively the Church and that the Patriarch of Rome is the head of and exercises authority over all Christians.

www.ingramcontent.com/pod-product-compliance
Lightning Source LLC
Chambersburg PA
CBHW070953040426
42443CB00007B/490